Tough Times,
Tight Times

Tough Times, Tight Times

WHAT CAN YOU DO?

Living, Surviving, and Thriving,
The Human Story
A Practical Guide for Saving Money on Energy, Food,
Clothing, and Everyday Necessities and
A Look at Finances and Health

SHARON P. (HAYDEN) BROWN, ED.D.

The opinions and ideas contained in this publication belong to the author and are intended to help individuals and families deal with economically challenging times. These "hard times" can come at any time but are especially prevalent in the latter part of 2000-2010. Legal, accounting or any other professional services discussed in this book should be sought by enlisting the advice and counsel of your own competent counselors or financial advisors before adopting financial suggestions from this book.

The author disclaims all responsibility for any liability, loss or risk, personal or otherwise, which is incurred as a consequence, directly, or indirectly, by the use and application of any of the contents of this book.

Illustrations drawn by Robert J. Cheseldine.

This book was printed in the United States of America.

To order additional copies of this book, contact:
Xlibris Corporation
1-888-795-4274
www.Xlibris.com
Orders@Xlibris.com
60074

Contents

Dedication

This book is dedicated to my mother, Cecilia M. (Battenfield) Hayden, and my father, Paul Cecil Hayden, who were both children of very large families during the Depression years in the 1930s. My mother was the ninth child of ten growing up in Washington DC. Food and its preparation was the heart of family gatherings, and she learned from her mother the art of using everything in the kitchen pantry and the "ice box" to prepare hearty and delicious meals. When she married and started her own family, she used this knowledge to stretch her dollar and to feed her husband and six children from the 1950s through the 1970s with just the salary of my father.

My father was the second child of eight and grew up in the rural southern part of Maryland in St. Mary's County. His mother planted a victory garden every year of her life, and she canned many vegetables and fruits for use during the winter months. In addition, my grandmother raised a cow, hogs, and chickens for their eggs, and of course, she used the chickens eventually for the dinner meat. Fried chicken was a Hayden family tradition every Sunday.

I would also like to dedicate this book to the wonderful women who were a part of my family's life while growing up in Annapolis, Maryland. My parents had friends who were hardworking, self-sacrificing, and aware of the meaning of living on a budget with every day being "tight times." Mrs. Elizabeth Early and her mother, Granny Smith, Mrs. Loretta McGee, Mrs. Ethel Mohr, Mrs. Marie Cullinan, and Mrs. Cecilia Gregory were all strong, wonderful role models for me and my siblings.

Lastly, I would like to dedicate this book to Gwen Pennington or Mrs. Juanita Abbott as I fondly knew her for many years. Juanita had six children and was a stay-at-home mom. She was extremely ingenious when searching for ways to feed and clothe her family and providing the many things they needed to manage a home.

Preface

This book is a labor of love and was written for several reasons. Over many years, I have observed the way in which families shop in our local grocery stores. Some families are not aware of the shopping practices that can potentially eat away their hard-earned dollar. The power of a dollar can be eroded as a consumer purchases processed and boxed food items that can be prepared just as easily for just pennies when you start from scratch using staples from your own pantry. For a long time, I have thought about the manner in which we could let people know some simple strategies to help them spend less money in the supermarket. The extra money left over from smart shopping could be spent on entertainment, luxuries, college educations for children and saving for a home.

Using common household food products, families can save a lot of money with just a few simple staples and the recipes that go with them. Most working parents are tired after a long day of work. I have developed a number of Crock-Pot recipes that when prepared early in the morning are ready to eat when the family arrives home in the evening.

As an educator over the past thirty-eight years working as a teacher, Title I coordinator, principal, and social worker, I have seen the plight of families in poverty or just plain, hardworking blue-collar laborers struggling to make ends meet for their families. This book is especially written for and dedicated to these average working-class people who pay their taxes and their mortgages and are the backbone of American society. I have developed this resource for families to assist them in further stretching their dollar.

Lastly, I wanted to share my ideas with my own family and give them ideas on the basics of being thrifty. Looking for ways to save in everyday living is important in order to make their weekly paycheck stretch on their sometimes limited budgets. In the long run, over a period of years, these practices will make money available for savings, retirement, education and the high-ticket purchases such as houses, vacations, and vehicles.

Acknowledgments

I want to thank Dr. Charles Ridgell who has taken the time to look at this manuscript in the last few months of its writing and assisted me in editing this document. Dr. Ridgell has been a colleague and friend for the past twenty years and has been a wonderful support system for me over my many years as an educator.

Second, I would like to thank Mr. Robert J. Cheseldine who took the time to make the illustrations for my cover and at the beginning of each chapter. Robert is a student at the University of Baltimore, and has been a family friend since he was a baby.

Lastly, but most importantly, I would like to thank my husband, Andy; my sons, Tommy, Brian, and Randy; and my daughter-in-law, Tanya, for all their continued love and support. I would also like to recognize my two grandchildren, Marley and Tripp, who are both lights of my life.

Introduction

I decided to write this book for several reasons. Through various roles in my professional career, I have been involved with families who have been in need of food, shelter or clothing. Beginning at Towson State College (currently known as Towson University) in the late 1960s, my first experience occurred when I was cochairman of the social committee for the women's residence halls. During the Christmas season each year, the social committee of women's residence halls organized a project to provide a party for needy children who lived in the poverty-stricken inner city of Baltimore City. The committee connected with the minister of a local Baltimore City church. He provided us a list of the names of one hundred children who would benefit by receiving gifts, time, and attention from someone outside their families during the holiday season. My job was to enlist the service of one hundred Towson volunteer students who would agree to participate, give their time, and buy a few gifts (a toy and an article of clothing) for the child with whom they would be partnered. We took several school buses from the college campus along with the special Towson buddies and picked up the needy children at the church. We then took the children and their partners back to the college campus for a Christmas party at the student center. At the end of the event, the children were given their age-appropriate presents by their "Christmas Towson student buddy." We all rode back to the church and then returned the children to their families at the church. This was one of my first experiences of actually seeing firsthand the poverty in our country and meeting up with it close and personal and seeing it in the faces of these children. I remember feeling a great sense of melancholy that night as we left the children, and I realized that these kids would return to their sometimes-hopeless situations of poverty.

Another experience in which I encountered the real faces of poverty came as I completed my student teaching in an inner city public school in Baltimore City off North Avenue. Prior to my first day of student teaching, I remember being told by the school staff that we should park our cars close to the building, and that we should come as a group and leave as a group. In addition, we were told to leave as soon as the day was over because of the potential for crime and violence in the neighborhood. Eight-foot chain-linked fences surrounded the playground around the outside of the building. Teachers told stories of how these children and families survived. I still remember feeling a great sense of compassion and empathy for these children that I worked with for three months. Each day, they came to school eager to learn. But I had such a sense of fear for them as they left the confines of the safety of our school walls and returned to their homes where they barely had enough in way of food, clothing, and shelter. Poverty has always existed, and I am not sure that we can change that completely. However, I do believe that there are some tips and practices that we can share with these families that may be helpful in making their lives economically less challenging with the little money that they do get each month.

The next time in my life when I had direct contact with families in poverty was through my positions as a Title I coordinator in four different schools from 1984 to 1989. Schools were designated as Title I by the percentage of free and reduced lunches that children received in the school. These schools were then entitled to extra money that was invested in human resources and extra materials in the hope that it would make a difference in the academic lives of these children and families. Again, I was actively involved in the midst of these family's hardships daily for four years. These families faced many challenges and problems as they dealt with and confronted poverty each day of their lives.

While in undergraduate school in the late 1960s, I was introduced to Maslow's hierarchy of needs in a social psychology class. It is a simple theory displayed in a pyramid diagram that tells the story of how we, as human beings, can reach our God-given potential of self-actualization. Maslow's theory explains how, until human beings have the very basic needs of food, clothing, and shelter, they will find it extremely difficult to reach each successive level of their goals of self-actualization (1954).

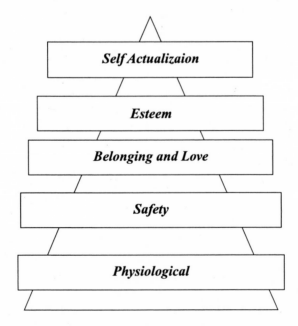

Pyramid of Maslow's Hierarchy of Basic Needs

So what does self-actualization really mean for children as they grow to adulthood?

- It means that a person has mastered the art of living in societal harmony as well as meeting all his personal goals and dreams.
- It means that a person has reached that state where he can look at a situation objectively as opposed to subjectively.
- It means that a person sees problems or challenges as opportunities requiring solutions.
- It means that a person enjoys privacy and finds solace in being alone.
- It means that a person forms his own opinions and judgments based on what he knows rather than following the group's thoughts.
- It means that a person feels comfortable being a nonconformist and is not pressured by the group's opinions.
- It means that a person realizes his talents and creativity and uses them.
- It means that a person exhibits social compassion and caring about humanity.
- It means that a person can be accepting of others without feeling the need to change people.
- It means that a person possesses an understanding of being democratic and is fair, nondiscriminating, and is capable of embracing and enjoying all cultures, races, and individual styles (Maslow 1968, 35).

Before self-actualization can occur, a person must first have his very basic needs met as outlined on the first levels of the pyramid. If a person does not have food, shelter, and clothing, he or she will most likely not be able to move up the varying levels of the triangle to ultimately reach the highest level of self-actualization. Though this theory is interpreted as being sequential, we all know those people who beat the odds and become self-actualized despite the many disadvantages they have along the way. However, I believe that it is essential that humans have the very basic needs of safety met to be able to access other parts of their human development.

This theory has many implications for our families today during these tough times. As financial markets have collapsed and unemployment has risen dramatically, many families have experienced bankruptcy and foreclosure and are homeless, renting or living in circumstances far different from what they have been accustomed to. Many food pantries across the country are seeing middle-class America knocking at their doors for the first time ever. These families are either on the edge of losing their homes or have already succumbed to this tragedy. Because so many families are seeking help, our food pantries across our country are beginning to experience difficulty in keeping up with the needs of their communities. Many charitable organizations are trying to keep their doors open to the poor and the families who may be experiencing temporary need. Increasingly, they are finding it difficult to provide these families with relief from their struggles. When families do not have the basics of food, shelter, and clothing—the first level of Maslow's pyramid—they cannot move to the next levels of this pyramid.

Another tremendous impact that poverty and the economic situation have on families is their children's ability to fully participate in school activities and access all the learning that is necessary for them to achieve their greatest levels of potential. We know that good nutrition is a factor in a child's healthy development. For this reason, many schools provide breakfast to children in schools which have met the criteria of being designated a Title I school (a certain percentage of free and reduced lunches). Through recent brain research in the last decade, we know that the brain works through the sugars or carbohydrates that are present in the body. Our brains have something called dendrites, which are like tiny wires or nerve endings. When the dendrites are stimulated by sugar, students' brains are making thought connections called synapses. In order for the thought processes to be completed, the dendrites must be fed sugars. If the brain is not fed by sugars (carbohydrates), these synapses will not occur. For this reason, it is extremely important that our children be fed a good breakfast each morning. This brain research provides the conclusive evidence of why, for years, educators have encouraged children to eat a good breakfast each day before they begin school and even, just as importantly, before our children enter into testing situations.

Our country today, because of the No Child Left Behind Act, holds teachers and schools accountable for children's learning through test scores, which are gained after a series of four or more days of spring testing. Based on Maslow's hierarchy of needs, I believe it is unfair to see the measures that are taken against a school, whose student populations experience a high level of poverty. As a factor of poverty, these students' circumstances may include a lack of food, shelter and clothing, and concerns about security and safety in their neighborhoods. If test scores do not meet the proposed standards, schools across our country face losing their principals and their entire staff of teachers. This situation is a travesty not only to the teachers but also to the students because these actions are based solely on the fact that the test scores did not meet adequate yearly progress. Schools may be making progress but will still be penalized because they haven't made a particular score. Oftentimes, in schools that are deemed as in "need of improvement," the educators have worked tirelessly to seek effective methods in helping each of their students to meet their God-given potential. Each day, these teachers walk through the doors of their schools. They work hard to make certain that not any of their students fall between the cracks and that these children are truly not left behind in our country as the federal government and politicians have mandated through the No Child Left Behind Act.

From a personal perspective, in February 2008, my son was laid off from his job as a project manager, supervising the construction of more than one hundred homes a year in an Atlanta construction company. He fell in the ranks of many families throughout this country as an unemployed citizen. During this period of "tight times," I came to the realization that his situation of tight times was temporary. In addition, he had the support of his extended family and the knowledge that he would again have a job in the future. And though, in this situation, our family was looking for ways to save a penny or a dollar today, we knew that eventually this situation would end and get better. It also struck me in a very profound way that because we knew our situation was temporary, we were able to hold on to *hope* that things would improve for us, and we would eventually experience a better tomorrow.

Unfortunately, some families and children in poverty never know the security of an adequate monthly income from the day they are born until the day they die. For them, "tight times" are every day of their lives. They never leave their situations and circumstances of poverty.

This book is especially dedicated to these strong, wonderful people who fight every day to exist and provide the best that they can for their children. I was able to see additionally the reality of the cycle of poverty during my three-year tenure as a middle school principal in a school where the poverty level was 45 %. The fact exists that these families do not have anyone to help them pay for schooling beyond high school in order to bring themselves out of this cycle of poverty. Many of my students expressed that they don't consider college because they believe the financial support of such schooling is beyond their means. Those of us in this country, who belong to the class of haves, cannot even begin to imagine how hopeless these situations present themselves for the families who live them daily. In our world market today, we know that the American workforce needs levels of education beyond high school in order to succeed in this country. At minimum, every child needs to obtain a high school diploma. We know that ideally, every child should have some degree beyond high school either in a technical skill or a four-year college in order to adequately provide for themselves and their families in the future. These generational poor families need some source of financial assistance or support in order to break this continual cycle of poverty.

Over the past fifteen years as an elementary and middle school principal, I have had the privilege of working with, helping, and knowing many families in poverty. I have thought about several ways in which each of us could assist these families in our communities. First, we are all fellow human beings (brothers and sisters) who are put on this earth for a short period of time. As we travel through and lead our lives, those of us who are blessed to have a home and many luxuries have a responsibility to reach out to those less fortunate. We can do this in many ways, and what a wonderful world it would be if everyone would reach out and help someone. I came up with a saying in the past several years as I have often thought about this topic.

"Each one, help one."

It is such a simple statement that means so much. Just four little words! Each person who is capable either by finances or time could help just one person or family in their immediate community. Through this single act of kindness, we could change our communities, our country, and ultimately our world.

As a school principal and a social worker for a Maryland school system, I have been privy to the personal lives of many families. Because of my role, families often shared their personal economic challenges through the years. Because of this knowledge, I have had the privilege of organizing and directing programs that could help these families in a small way.

Being a member of the Rotary Club of Charlotte Hall in Maryland from 1994-2003, I had connections with community members that were willing to help me with food for some of our families who were in dire need from time to time. I will never forget a young mother of four children who came to my office one day to talk to me about her hardship of not having enough food for her family. In one month's time, because her husband was out of work, she confided in me that one of her children had lost seven pounds. In our country right now, we have many families, known as the working poor, who are in the same circumstances. As members of our communities, we have the responsibility to reach out and help those we know who are in need especially if we have the means to do so.

For ten years, when I was principal at Lettie Marshall Dent Elementary School in Mechanicsville, Maryland, we delivered Thanksgiving baskets of food to our needy families through the generosity of our school parents, the PTA, the Charlotte Hall Rotary Club, SMECO (Southern Maryland Electric Company), our school staff, and the local churches. At Christmas, many children woke up to a brighter holiday as a result of the generosity and efforts of these same groups of people. As our country faces the current economic crisis and challenge, we must all reach out and help in the ways that we can. One of my professors at the University of Maryland once said to me that most of us are just a couple of paychecks away from being homeless. It is a very frightening time, and I hope that this book, in some small way, will help families know that they are not alone in their struggles and that there are resources that are at their fingertips to help them stretch their dollar and their budget.

References

Maslow, A. 1954. *Motivation and personality*. New York: Harper.

Maslow, A. 1968. *Toward a psychology of being*. 2nd ed. New York: Van Nostrand Reinhold.

What did you do for clothing?

"My father worked for fifty-five years in a general store from 6:00 a.m. until 11:00 p.m., from 1921 until 1976, just two years before he died at the age of eighty. My father brought the flour and feed sacks home from the general merchandise store. These sacks were made out of colorful cotton fabric. Using an old Singer sewing machine with pedals, my mother made broomstick skirts and blouses for my sisters, pillowcases, blankets, and quilts.

"In the summer, children went barefoot and reserved their shoes for school and the winter months."

In what ways did children entertain themselves during these tight times?

"My Uncle Tillie and Uncle Howard would take us to the movies in Leonardtown. We also went to the church hall, and we would roller-skate for hours. Kids would play with puzzles and play card games.

"On Sundays, my parents would make homemade ice cream in the old hand-cranked ice cream machines. We all took turns cranking the machine for about an hour before it was finished. This was such a treat for our family."

What are some other things that you remember about growing up in the Depression?

"We had a general store that provided almost anything families would need. You could buy shoes, nonprescription medicine, food, fresh meats, fruits and vegetables, yard goods and garden supplies, vegetable and flower seeds, feed for the animals, fertilizer, penny candy, liquor, gasoline, and automotive supplies. The general store also served as the post office for the community.

"When families needed the services of a doctor, they didn't always have money to pay the doctor. Oftentimes, they were paid by bartering with meats, hams, chickens, butter, sausage, eggs, and other food items. During these times when things were tight, even doctors were very appreciative of these items.

"My mother made our mattresses, blankets, and pillows from the feathers of the chickens. I remember that the blankets were very heavy.

"My Uncle Tillie made wooden chairs that sat out on our porch as well as all the porches of our neighbors on Abell Road."

My Mother's Story during the Depression Years

Presently, my mother, Cecilia M. (Battenfield) Hayden, is eighty-three and lives in Annapolis, Maryland. She was born on May 2, 1926, which was six years before the stock market crash. My mother grew up in the city of Washington DC, on Sixteenth and

A Street in Southeast DC. I interviewed my mother in November of 2008 and asked her some questions that would help me understand what it was like for her family during the Depression in the 1930s. My mother was the ninth child in her family, and her household consisted of nine brothers and sisters (Helen, Bill [Buck], Charlotte [Pumpy], John [Juggy], Mabel [Tudi], Joe [Hop], Frances [Frannie], Eileen [Leni], and Teresa), her mother, and father.

Do you remember the day that the stock market crashed and what happened during the Depression?

"I was six so I don't remember specifically what happened on that day. My father was a painter, and I do remember that as times became tight with the Depression, painting was one of the first services that people would do without during those tight times. My grandfather owned one of the busiest interior-decorating businesses in Washington DC, specializing in painting, draperies, and upholstering. My father worked for my grandfather at their J. E. Battenfield House and Fresco Painting interior-decorating business, which was located at 738 Thirteenth Street NW. Their family business was lost in 1933 because of the Depression. Up until that time, they had contracts regularly working around the city and particularly in the United States Capitol, painting walls and repairing wood trim."

How did your parents provide for the necessities of food and clothing?

"My mother would go to the market downtown at Fifth and K Street NW to buy bread. Every day, my mother would fix a pot of soup. She would take whatever was leftover from the day before to make the soup. Large families worked together during these tight times. I had several brothers and sisters who had graduated from high school, and they would contribute money each week to the running of the household. My mother and father had a budget, and my mother was given a certain amount of money for food, and that is all that she would spend. My mother would buy our food at the local market on the corner of our street. The market would keep a running bill, and my mother would pay it off at the end of the week when my father would get paid. Sometimes, we would buy food at the larger Safeway store in our community.

"With ten children, many pairs of shoes had to be purchased each year. If our shoes got a hole in them, my father would repair the shoes by putting on new rubber soles with glue. He had a steel foot in the basement, and he would use this to repair the shoes. Sometimes, we would cut out a piece of cardboard and put it on the inside of our shoe to cover a hole. My mother would take the trolley to downtown DC several times a year, and she would purchase a bag full of shoes off the rack of a department store. When she got home, she would dump the bag out on the floor, and whomever the shoes fit, that is what they wore.

"Because we had a large family, I remember once that the church sent over a basket of food. My mother was a very proud woman, and she wouldn't accept it. It upset her so much. I remember that she was fussing with my father and saying, 'I'm not taking that. I'm not that bad off, take that back!'

"To save money, my mother made our clothes. She would buy the fabric at the big department stores downtown when it was on sale. I particularly remember Kann's department store."

In what ways did children entertain themselves during these tight times?

"When I was little, we never went anywhere away from the city. However, on Saturday nights, we would go to the movies at Eastern High School on East Capital Street. The charge for admission was a nickel. I remember they would often show serials that would go from week to week. Movies were a common entertainment in those times.

"We lived in an end row house, and we would play in the alley in the back of our home. It was our playground, and we especially liked to play baseball, basketball, and dodge ball. We also entertained ourselves with the game of jacks and hopscotch. Life before the Depression was known as the Roaring Twenties."

What are some other things that you remember about growing up in the Depression?

"We never had a car growing up. We walked a lot, and we occasionally used the bus or trolley/streetcar for transportation. Once in a while, my mother would take us to the big department stores, such as Woodies, Kann's, the Hecht Company, and Lansberg.

"My father kept a safe in our dining room. He would keep the money in the safe, and when my mother would need something, he would get the money out of the safe. My mother did not use credit. She did use the layaway plan, and the items would stay in the store until she could pay them off.

"We also used to have lots of door-to-door salesmen. I remember that we bought products from a company called Watkins. The Watkins salesman would sell products like milk and bread each week."

My Story Growing Up in the Hayden Home

When I was a child growing up in Annapolis, Maryland, we always had what we needed as kids. By this, I mean, we had the basics of food, shelter, and clothing. My parents were determined to give us a Catholic education. Consequently, they worked hard to prepare a weekly budget that permitted them to have enough money to send all six of their children to St. Mary's Catholic School in Annapolis. They did without a lot of luxuries in order to provide us with what they felt was the most important thing they could give us. That was an excellent education that was wrapped around the strong Christian/Catholic beliefs that our family possessed. Our Catholic tradition had been passed on from many past generations. We were given the toys and books that were appropriate for children, but nothing in comparison to what we have seen given to children over the past thirty years. Today's parents feel they need to provide their children with everything that comes on the market. One underused resource available to families everywhere is a public library.

Reading books has always been a cherished pastime for me. I have fond memories of my first trip to the public library in Annapolis with my father in 1954. The trip was special for several reasons and remains in my mind as a vivid memory even all these years later. First, growing up in a large family, time with our parents by ourselves was rare. So this trip with my father by myself without my brother or sister was special in my eyes as a child. Second, the occasion was special because I had turned six and had now reached the age where I could have my very own library card. Third, the place in which the children's section was housed seemed like an adventure and mystery to me because it was housed in the basement of this four-story historic building. Accessibility to the children's section could be obtained only by going down an outside stairwell. As we entered through the outside door, my first memory was one of awe. I remember gazing upon all those many bookshelves stacked full of books just inviting me to take part in their wonderful adventures of make-believe, reality, or fantasy.

Over the many years from first through twelfth grade, I remember walking up Duke of Gloucester Street in Annapolis to the public library. Later, in high school, I would make this walking trip from the public high school through the many backstreets with the beautiful Annapolis's historic homes. I would complete this routine three or four times a week and my father would pick me up after work on these days. Today, families do not nearly use free public resources such as the library as much as they could. People frequent media and bookstores and spend a fortune for books, DVDs, CDs, or videos. *By using the public library, you can save thousands of dollars throughout the year on books, videos, DVDs, CDs, and computers if you don't have the budget to purchase these items.*

Another outing or activity that was always fun for me and my sisters was centered on the chore of weekly supermarket shopping. With six children in the family, a shopping trip was necessary by the end of each week. My mother worked hard as a homemaker to provide us with good meals and clothes to wear each day. She had a budget and always lived within the boundaries of that budget. My mother sewed all of her clothes as well as her three daughters' clothing. On Thursday nights, we would do the weekly grocery shopping as well as run any errands we needed to accomplish for the coming week. We had one car that my father used to transport himself to work during the day, so my mother planned the trips that we made in the evening when he came home. Typically, stores ran their sale ads from Wednesday through Tuesday. My mother would go through the ads and buy the items we needed that were on sale. She would also clip any coupons that might be available. Our trip often involved a neighbor who came along with us. I remember making a trip to the local five-and-dime store, singing songs in the car and topping the trip off with a stop at the local drugstore. It is amazing that something as simple as stopping by a local drugstore to get an ice cream soda could be the highlight of the week. For me, this weekly excursion has remained a lifelong memory.

Today's parent believes that children need to have extravagant vacations or excursions when really all they need is the gift of your time over something as simple as an ice cream cone. If we think back through our lives, pricey vacations, gifts, and toys are not the things we remember. It is the time and love shared with our families and friends during our growing-up days as children.

The Brown Family's Recent Story

Recently, our family has experienced firsthand what economic hard times are doing to young families across our country. Our eldest son was employed as a project manager in a housing construction company in Atlanta, Georgia. His responsibilities included bringing over one hundred homes a year to completion from start to finish. This past year, his company saw a huge economic slowdown in the number of new homes being constructed. He was laid off along with sixteen other employees in February 2008. His economic contribution to the family income was completely eliminated. Additionally, his status as the primary breadwinner was now reversed. His wife became the person who left each day for work while his role was reversed as the caretaker of two preschoolers, the chief cook, and bottle washer. I have watched in such awe at the manner in which both he and my daughter-in-law have responded to their very difficult situation. I am incredibly proud of them. To date, their children have little knowledge of the hardships in which their parents found themselves. Consequently, the children have weathered this storm quite well.

As parents find themselves in these role reversals through no fault or choice of their own, it is imperative for husbands and wives to find the time to discuss their problems, circumstances, and the possible solutions. These discussions should preferably take place in the absence of their children. Children will not understand the stress that their parents are experiencing and may become anxious if exposed to the many daily stresses that unemployment brings. Children's routines should continue in order to maintain normalcy and consistency.

What are some of the positives that men can discover when they find themselves unemployed? For one, men have an opportunity to give their children the gift of quality time every day they are home. Typically, men do not stay home to take care of the children and the home. You may ask, "How can you view the loss of your job as an opportunity and even a blessing?" As the traditional roles between the father going to work and the mother staying at home are reversed, the man has a chance to spend time with his children and perform parental duties, which are not typically performed by the father. The strong relationship that he can build with his children during this time is something that money will never buy. The memories will be lifelong.

Strong Nurturing Women Who Have Influenced My Life

In 1954, when I was five, my father was transferred to Annapolis, Maryland, for his job in a telephone company. My family moved into our new home in the community of Victor Haven, a small subdivision in Annapolis. In the mid 1950's, these new homes were sold for $11,000. The American dream of owning a home was made possible for many people during that period of American history. It is from these families as well as my own that I have learned so much about being thrifty, honest, respectful, hardworking, and being a good citizen of your community. Additionally, my personal commitment to volunteerism and giving back to my community came from watching and observing my mother, father, and neighbors give so much to each other in their times of need and crisis. Over those next seven years, I was a part of this small community where adults embraced their children and families supported each other through the everyday trials and tribulations of just plain living. My mom had many friends; some were connected through their mutual faith and devotion to the Catholic Church, and some shared the same family values that she had. I was very fortunate to have been a part of this era and to learn so much about life from these women who were the rocks of their families. I have written the stories of these women as a tribute to them and the beautiful lives they have led. They have always been and will continue to be a source of inspiration to me.

<u>Ethel's Story</u>

Ethel and her two children, Barbara and Dickey, lived in the house to the right of us. She had four children, two from the first marriage and two from the second marriage. Her first husband had passed away, and her second husband had left years earlier; and she was raising her two youngest children by herself. Her eldest son had been killed in World War II. To this day, I can remember the picture of her son in uniform, which sat on top of her television, just like it was yesterday. Her second son was married and had two children. Ethel was a storyteller, and I remember her teaching me many lessons over the years when we were neighbors. I remember that she worked hard outside of the home as a single mother to provide for her children. She never knew times that were not tight.

Ethel did not always live next door to us. As a renter, she moved several times over a period of twenty years. Our family remained friends through the four or five homes that she rented. I will never forget the time when my mother and I dropped by to see Ethel who was then living in a town house in Eastport. Our visits were never announced because we had such a comfortable friendship. When we arrived at her home, Dickey was not there, and my mother asked about his whereabouts. As a child, when I heard that they had no food in the house and Dickey was out in the neighborhood selling his toys in order to buy a can of soup, I was horrified. It was at that moment that I understood what true poverty meant. As a child, I could not imagine not having a single bite of food in the house. Of course, my mother, being the generous and compassionate person that she is, went home and put together several bags of groceries to bring to Ethel and her family.

Over the years, Ethel and her family were frequently part of our Thanksgiving family celebrations. At my home, I loved the fact that this holiday was shared with friends and other families that might not have as much as we did. My mother taught me from a very young age to act on the knowledge that someone else is hurting or has some very basic needs in which you can help.

Ethel and her two children are no longer living today, but I will always remember the financial struggles that they faced from time to time through their lives. She was a survivor, and she made do with what she had. Not surprisingly, she was a very proud woman and never complained about her circumstances. When I think of Ethel now, my memories are of a woman with a very hearty laugh and sense of humor that was never ending.

Loretta's Story

Loretta lived two doors down from us in our community of Victor Haven. She raised three children (Terry, Penny, and Ricky) by herself due to the untimely death of her husband who was just thirty-four years old. Her husband was in the military, and one evening, he lay down on the sofa after work and never woke up. He had a massive heart attack, and this happened after having gone for an annual checkup the day before and being declared in good health.

Loretta was a survivor. She got a job at the Anne Arundel General Hospital in Annapolis and worked there most of her life until she retired. Her life changed when her husband passed away. She made many sacrifices in order that her children could have a Catholic education. When I look back now, I do not know how she did it, but somehow she survived. I remember one clever practice related to Christmas that she did every year but was certainly outside of the tradition of how the majority of Americans celebrate this holiday. In order to make her dollar stretch, she would purchase one small item for each of her three children to be opened on Christmas Day. The next day, she would take her children to the shopping mall for the after-Christmas sales, and they would then purchase items at a highly reduced price. When the monetary funds were limited, this was an excellent way for her children to be able to purchase needed clothing as well as a few toys.

Marie's Story

Marie raised four children (Sharon, Ricky, Robert, and Cathy) in a house around the corner from us in Victor Haven. She also was a stay-at-home mother and made ends meet on the salary of her husband who served in the navy. After taking care of her own children for many years, she ran a day care business in her home to make extra money in order to make ends meet. She also was a devoted mother and wife. Marie also had a deep love of her Catholic faith. She always seemed to be a beacon of strength in whatever challenge that might come her way. She loved her children, and her conversation constantly revolved around them. She and my mother remained friends for over fifty years until her death a few years back. In later years as I visited Marie, her conversations centered around her children and grandchildren and they continued to remain at the center of her world. What an inspiration and model for all of us women who became mothers!

Elizabeth's Story

Elizabeth lived in the house next door to us. After Ethel moved to another community, she moved into the house that Ethel had vacated. Elizabeth also raised four children (Kenny, Tommy, Danny, and Jimmy). Raising four boys can be very challenging, but she always did it with grace and the most wonderful sense of humor. Her laugh was contagious. I remember how devoted Elizabeth was to her Catholic faith and how much care and attention she gave to her mother, Granny Smith, as she was affectionately known to all the kids in the neighborhood. Elizabeth was such a wonderful role model for all the children that surrounded her. She was a devoted mother and wife. She also raised her family on a limited budget from her husband's salary as an owner of a small TV repair business. Because Elizabeth used her knowledge of thrifty practices to make ends meet, she was able to stay at home to raise her four children.

Juanita's Story

Forty years ago, I met a woman by the name of Juanita. Juanita was bigger than life in a very ordinary way. She represented the everyday America where women and men meet the challenges of raising a family in our country. Juanita was married to a teacher, and by the mid to late '70s, they had six children. Juanita, a domestic engineer, was very creative and ingenious in making her dollar stretch on her husband's teacher salary. She used coupons regularly. She prepared meals that were not costly. Occasionally, they ate hot dogs. Hot dogs are not the most nutritional meal. Juanita didn't have the money to buy expensive cuts of meat or fresh fruits and vegetables every day. She needed to feed a family of eight and she did what she had to do in order to make ends meet.

Juanita was very active in her church. Sunday morning and Wednesday evening services were a must for her family. I cannot remember a time when she did not have all of her kids dressed, fed, and ready to go. She instilled in her children good Christian values.

Juanita was ahead of her times as a female who dappled in carpentry work from time to time. Once, I remember her building two extra bedrooms in the basement of her one-story home to give her teenage daughters and sons more privacy.

Somehow, Juanita always seemed to know when a good deal was happening in our community. I remember a time when she called me to tell me that the Golden Corral restaurant was buying new chairs for their dining area, and they were selling the old

shelter, and to have the means to get to work. She feels let down that our economy has gotten this bad in a country that she feels knows better than to get themselves into this situation. She believes that the citizens of the United States knew we were in a recession before our president ever admitted it. She believes the housing, job, and stock markets are all in need of major restructuring.

She has a longtime friend who has worked for forty-two years for Circuit City as a district manager. The company has gone bankrupt and does not want to give him his benefits and pay for which he has worked all his life. He is just one of many thousands of people who are facing the same scenario across our nation.

Marie feels that we have been living in a bubble since the 1980s, and it had to burst. She sees better times ahead, but not the same as the past three decades. Marie believes it will be harder to become "rich," and the middle class will grow only if jobs are brought back to the United States. She believes that banks, insurance companies, health care, private companies, mortgage lenders, and credit companies should be more regulated and in the future, the public will demand that businesses become more "transparent" than in the past.

Marie believes we will all be expected to understand and utilize technology in our jobs and our everyday lives. We will work smarter and find more efficient ways to complete tasks. Our country will be compelled to think globally to remain competitive in the world markets. Schools in the United States will need to focus once again on more science and mathematics programs in order to produce more inventors, scientists, and logical/mathematical thinkers.

Marie also thinks that our country needs to focus on bringing back jobs to the United States so that we are not importing so many products from foreign countries. Politicians need to focus on ways to support and encourage the development of alternative forms of fuel and energy.

Finally, Marie believes that better times are in the forecast if we are willing to look at what is or is not working globally. She believes that we all need to take accountability for our actions and make decisions that will benefit everyone, not just personal selfish needs and motives. The federal government needs to work with state and county levels of government throughout our country to develop more universal approaches to financial, health care, and environmental issues.

Kathleen, Teacher and Graduate Student

Kathleen says during tight times, there is no disposable income for things such as vacations or movies. She has always had tight times since she has been a divorced, single mother who has managed to raise her two sons, work two jobs, and put herself through undergraduate and graduate school. She has had to plan ahead for everything and only has financial resources for the necessities. Over the years, she has had constant stress and worry.

Her sons are grown now—one still in college and one who has just completed college and is seeking employment. She has not been able to help her children a lot financially, consequently, they have learned to settle for what they need and not what they want. She has always bought clothing on sale and frequents thrift shops for bargains.

To make ends meet, she does not go out to eat very often. She prepares meals that freeze well. She plans her shopping list around foods that are seasonal and on sale. She drinks water from her tap and doesn't buy sodas. She turns down the thermostat in the winter, wears more layers of clothing, and uses more blankets at night. She does not use air-conditioning if at all possible.

To reduce her fuel intake, Kathleen plans her errands so that she stops on her way to or from work each day. She does not take leisure trips and is able to make one tank of gas last for two weeks. Two years ago, she purchased a Toyota Corolla to replace her old car. Her new car now gets thirty miles to a gallon of gasoline.

To conserve energy, Kathleen uses electricity only when appliances are in use. If not in use, she turns off lights, computers, monitors, television, cable boxes, etc. She keeps the thermostat at sixty-five degrees in the winter and seventy-eight degrees in the summer. When she does have to replace something in the house, she makes sure its replacement is efficient. Kathleen recycles paper, plastic, and glass.

Because Kathleen started her career at forty-five, the economic turmoil has had a greater impact on her. She has no retirement other than the one from work. She can only afford to put away $25 a pay period because she is in the lower end of the pay scale. Kathleen figures that she will not be able to retire until she is seventy. She worries about health issues and not being able to work. She feels constant stress and, as a result, is always tired.

Kathleen sees better times for her children because they have earned their four-year degrees in higher education at a younger age. She hopes that they will not have to struggle as she has had to do her whole life. Kathleen will continue to take more classes after her master's degree in order for her to move to the upper end of the pay scale and to be able to save more money toward her retirement.

Tracie, Music Teacher

Tight times to Tracie means living from paycheck to paycheck. She asks herself whether a purchase is really necessary and whether it is a want or a need.

Recently, Tracie's husband lost his job because his employer did not have enough money to pay him. Her husband has found a job, but it involves a total of a two-hour commute each day. Tight times for Tracie mean purchasing only the grocery-store brands. They bought a new home in the spring of 2008 and could not sell their first home. They have been paying two mortgages for over a year.

To make ends meet, Tracie buys only store brands for everything from food to paper towels. She and her husband do not go out to dinner or the movies. She goes to the library to check out movies for free. While taking one of her master's degree classes, she had to borrow the textbook from a friend.

Tracie's family reduces their fuel costs by sharing rides to work and making only one trip to the store to complete errands at the end of the week.

To conserve energy, Tracie sets her thermostat to seventy-five degrees in the summer and sixty-eight degrees in the winter.

For Tracie, it is hard to be focused so constantly on money and monitoring her bank accounts so carefully.

Tracie sees hope for the future because she just doesn't believe that things will stay bad forever.

Carrie, Elementary School Teacher

Tight times for Carrie imply a temporary situation. She believes that it is a struggle for families to maintain their lifestyles, and they are forced to cut back on extra spending.

Carrie is single and has a roommate to help her pay the mortgage. Winter heating bills present a challenge and sometimes cause her to use a credit card to make ends meet.

To make ends meet, Carrie has cut off her trash service, cable TV, and Internet service. She eats meals at home and tries to find ways to cook for one on a budget. She has taken an extra job by tutoring in an after-school reading program in order to earn extra cash. She finds it difficult to eat cheap and maintain her health and diet.

To save money on gasoline, Carrie travels less to her friends' and relatives' houses. Though it is free to stay at these places once she arrives, the fuel to get there makes it impossible to travel.

In order to conserve energy, Carrie turns off the lights when leaving a room and turns off the computer when it is not in use. She has her thermostat set at sixty-six degrees during the winter and seventy-two degrees for the cooling during the summer months. She has begun to replace major appliances and light bulbs with updated and energy-efficient models.

For Carrie, the economic turmoil causes personal stress and constant underlying worry about making the bills and cutting back debt. The economic situation has caused stress in her relationships with her boyfriend, parents, brother, and sometimes friends.

She believes that the future will get better but that it will take a fifteen-year period.

Jenny, Food Service Manager at an Elementary School

For Jenny, tight times mean a lack of money. You have to stretch your dollar. She does not go out that much anymore. Jenny and her husband rarely eat out. To get rid of things that have accumulated throughout the year, she and her husband have two annual yard sales—one in the winter and one in the spring. Since most of her clothing and household items have been purchased at previous yard sales, she is able to get back all of her money invested the year before; and sometimes, she actually makes a couple of extra dollars.

To help make ends meet, Jenny burns her fireplace every day. When she walks the dog, she collects kindling and branches from the woods in her backyard. Jenny rarely buys anything at a department store. She frequents her local thrift store on Wednesdays because purchases made on this day are half price. She thinks it is foolish to spend money on new things when you can buy the same product in excellent condition at a thrift store. She buys her husband's T-shirts for $.50 on Wednesdays at the Salvation Army thrift store. Jenny and her husband pick up videos because they never go to the movies. Additionally, Jenny shops at bazaars, flea markets, and a secondhand shop, which sponsors Habitat for Humanity. Recently, Jenny and her husband bought an oak staircase for $140, which had an estimated price of $900 if purchased new.

Jenny believes in bartering. She is a hairdresser by trade. She has bartered her services for things such as computer repairs, electrical advice, and the use of her sister's condo in Ocean City. Her husband has bartered his service of landscaping services for an additional electrical panel needed for a new air conditioner and a heating system.

Jenny doesn't believe in wasting food. She believes in the saying, "Waste not, want not." If she has ham leftovers, she prepares a ham casserole. If she has chicken leftovers, she makes chicken soup for dinner the next day. She purchases bulk items such as laundry detergent and toilet paper at BJ's.

To conserve electricity, her family keeps one light on. They have even been known to use a flashlight as they move through the house. Even with these extreme measures, her electric bill was $450 last month.

Jenny conserves energy and practices going green in many ways. Before Jenny goes to yard sales on Saturdays, she maps out a route for her trips in order to save money on gas. After preparing food at her school, she rinses the cans and brings them home to her recycle bin. She has never purchased new furniture. She uses Craigslist to buy secondhand items. In addition, she belongs to the group on www.freecycle.com where people advertise things they are trying to get rid of for free.

The economic downturn makes Jenny feel angry and upset. She believes that our nation has gotten ourselves into this predicament because our government was not keeping watch. She doesn't understand the country's priorities of paying football players fifty million dollars a year.

Jenny hopes that the economy straightens up, but she would like to see our boys/soldiers come home first. She doesn't see things straightening out anytime soon in the future. She says, "I will believe it when I see it."

Colleen, Youth Minister for a Catholic High School

Colleen says that dealing with tight times means staying on a budget in order to pay your bills. The budget includes just the basic needs. It means not having disposable income to buy extras. She has to wait to buy the extras or not buy them at all.

Her family works together during tight times. They have what they need but not always what they want.

To make ends meet during these economically challenging times, Colleen is shopping for sale items and using coupons. Her meals are planned around the food ads each week. Colleen does not eat out, and she packs her lunch every day for work. In the winter, she keeps the heat at sixty-eight degrees during the day and sixty-five degrees at night.

In order to save money on gas, Colleen no longer makes separate trips to the store. She shops on her way home from work. When the price of gasoline went up, money was no longer available for food and clothing. Fuel was necessary in order to get to work, so she had to cut back on the food budget. Her daughter took metro to work to Washington DC instead of driving her car.

Colleen engages in the practice of going green and conserving the environment by recycling all plastic, aluminum cans, and newspapers. She doesn't buy bottled water in order to conserve the use of plastic. Her family drinks water out of the faucet. Colleen uses cold water to wash clothes and turns off the lights in rooms that are not being used. She uses reusable cloth shopping bags to avoid the use of plastics.

During these tight times, her family realizes that they are blessed because they have jobs and are able to provide for themselves. She has seen a lot of families lose their jobs and could possibly lose their homes. The situation has made her family not take for granted what they do have.

Colleen sees hope for the future. She thinks that during these tight times, people are becoming more aware of their budgets and learning how to save money wisely. With the same salary, she believes one person might live like a king while the other lives like a pauper. It all has to do with being wise with your money. She remembers a story that her friend tells about a shopping trip to Marshalls with her teenage son. Her son was embarrassed and wanted to "get out of the store before someone saw him." The mother replied to her son, "You know a man never got rich by spending all of his money." Colleen thought this was a great lesson for a teenage boy.

Anonymous A

Tight times for A means no money to spare and "stress." It means sacrificing luxury items such as going out to dinner and the movies. She does not take long trips to avoid high gas prices. A has considered cutting out extra bills like Internet and the cell phone.

To help make ends meet, A does not buy unneeded items. She keeps a grocery list, which matches the money she has delegated in her budget. She does not use her car as much, and she avoids weekend trips.

In order to conserve energy and preserve the environment, A turns off the lights and recycles as much as possible.

Emotionally, A feels short of breath when she thinks about debt. She feels trapped by the confinement of her budget.

A does not see better times for the future. A believes that society tends to spend more and more. We tend to measure our success by our material possessions. Few people have learned to save, and more people spend money by using credit cards.

Anonymous B

B says that tight times mean financial constraints in regard to household necessities versus "what I would like to have."

For her family, tight times mean less entertainment options and the ability to afford the clothing of choice for her teenage boys.

To make ends meet during these economically challenging times, B is not going out to eat or the movies. She is making due with what she already has.

In order to save money on gas, B takes fewer trips to visit family members out of town. She is combining trips to the grocery store and other stores. She carpools in order to share transportation costs with other parents who have to pick up teenagers from after-school activities.

To conserve energy, she recycles and turns off appliances when they are not in use.

B says that the economical turmoil causes her to worry, which leads to stress.

Anonymous C

C says that tight times mean thinking about money, budgeting, compromising, and prioritizing. It means less luxuries, vacations, buying clothing, and eating out.

To make ends meet during these economically challenging times, C eats at home more. She is much thriftier when she shops at the grocery store, and she buys only what she needs and items that are on sale.

In order to save money on gas, C takes fewer vacations. She also carpools to go to activities.

To preserve the environment, C recycles everything in the area of plastics and paper.

C is unsure about the future. She is trying to consolidate debt, find ways to reduce her interest rates, and save money for college expenses.

C sees hope for the future but not anytime soon. She believes that nothing changes fast, and it will take time.

Helping Children Cope with Stress during Tight Times

Many families are experiencing economically challenging times across our country. Children will be faced with a variety of challenges such as follows:

- Seeing their mother or father lose a job
- Seeing their home being taken by the bank due to foreclosure or bankruptcy

Chapter 2

Shopping and Everyday Cooking

Waste not, want not

This chapter particularly discusses the ways in which you can save money at the grocery store and how to prepare economical meals. It outlines topics such as basic ingredients that families should have in their pantries, the use of leftovers, freezing leftovers, tips to avoid practices which are not economical, easy recipes for the Crock-Pot, recipes that use economical ingredients, places to buy food at cost-saving prices, and using and managing coupons for the grocery store.

What's in Your Pantry?
The Basic Ingredient List
Required for a Pantry at All Times

In order to have ingredients on hand at all times for everyday cooking needs, you should keep some basic supplies such as dry goods, fresh vegetables and fruits, canned goods, spices, dairy products, cooking oils, and pastas in your pantry and refrigerator. Oftentimes, as you begin to prepare a meal, you may find yourself wanting to use leftovers for an additional meal. For example, you may have a couple pieces of chicken in the refrigerator from the night before. You can debone it and use it in a stir-fry with onions, celery, carrots, and green pepper. If you have seasonal vegetables on hand such as squash or zucchini, you can slice these and add them to the stir-fry. You can make rice to go along with this, and you have an economical meal.

In order to make the most efficient use of your budget, always buy the *vegetables and fruits* for your family that are *in season* at the time of your purchase. Purchasing strawberries in the winter will be much more expensive than buying them in May and June. By refraining from buying fruits or vegetables out of season, you can save a tremendous amount of money when you view it over the period of a year.

When buying meats or any other food products at the grocery store, you should look for those products, which are on sale. I have seen filet mignon from $5.99 a pound to $15.99 a pound depending upon the market from where you buy it. When feeding a family of four, buying beef at $15.99 a pound versus $5.99 a pound could add up to a lot of unnecessary money being spent in your meat budget. Multiply this amount of your meat budget by two-hundred days, and you can see a significant cost differential.

The following list of basic ingredients should always be available in your pantry or refrigerator. (For extra copies, see appendix D.)

Pantry List

Dry Goods	Fruits
• Flour and Bisquick • Granulated Sugar, Brown sugar, and Confectioners • Corn Meal • Oatmeal	• Apples • Lemons • Bananas • Seasonal Fruit • Raisins
Vegetables	**Canned Vegetables**
• Potatoes • Onions • Celery • Carrots • Green Peppers	• Diced Tomatoes (1 lb and 2 lb) • Tomato Sauce (8 oz and 16 oz) • Tomato Paste • Cream of Mushroom Soup • Cream of Chicken Soup • Tomato Soup
Spices	**Dairy**
• Salt/Pepper • Baking Powder/Baking Soda • Bouillon Cubes (Beef and Chicken) • Seasoned Salt • Vinegar • Dry Onion Soup Mix	• Butter (Off-brand Acceptable) • Eggs • Sliced American Cheese • Block Sharp Cheese • Milk
Oils	**Pasta and Dried Beans**
• Olive Oil • Canola Oil • Spray Pam • Crisco/Shortening	• Vermicelli, Spaghetti, Linguine • Elbow Macaroni, Shells, Bowties, Twists • Dried Beans (Lima, Navy, Kidney, Split Pea, Northern Bean, Barley) • Rice (Brown and White)
Meats	**Desserts**
• Hot Dogs • Canned Tuna • Canned Chicken • Frozen Chicken • Frozen Hamburger	• Pudding/Jell-O • Graham Crackers/Vanilla Wafers • Ice Cream • Cool Whip • Animal Crackers
Frozen Vegetables	**Staples**
• Peas • Green Beans (Cut and French Style) • Corn • Spinach	• Peanut Butter • Mustard • Jelly • Ketchup

Processed Foods

Processed foods are very expensive since someone else is preparing them, and part of their profit is contained in the price of the item. One packaged processed food item can cost as much as it would cost to feed an entire family of four or five. Eliminating processed food items from your supermarket list can greatly reduce the overall cost of your weekly groceries. Let's take a look at how this works with just a few items.

Processed Food	Cost/Serving	Unprocessed Food	Cost/Serving
Oatmeal (prepackaged)	$3.44 (12 serv)	Quaker Oatmeal (oz)	$4.06 (30 serv)
Macaroni and Cheese	$1.06 (1 serv)	Pasta/Cheese/Milk/Butter	$1.10 (2 serv)
Pudding (4 packs)	$2.00 (4 serv)	Pudding	$1.24 (4 serv)
Pancake Mix	$2.57 (2 lb)	Pancakes from Scratch	$1.16 (2 lb)
Jell-O (4 packs)	$1.60	Jell-O	$0.89
Applesauce (6 packs)	$2.52 (24 oz)	Applesauce (48-oz jar)	$2.85 (48 oz)
Brown Rice (minute)	$2.51 (9 serv)	Brown Rice (2-lb bag)	$1.98 (22 serv)
Mashed Potatoes (instant)	$1.89 (3 cups)	Mashed Potatoes (whole potatoes)	$1.00 (3 cups)
Biscuits	8 for $1.99	Homemade Biscuits	14 for $0.50
Muffins	$1.50 each	Homemade Muffins	12 for $2.00

Not only are processed foods more expensive when you compare serving for serving, but they are oftentimes less nutritious for your family. Many products contain additional unnecessary fats and sugars.

Lunch

Packing your own lunch is much more economical than purchasing your meal at a fast-food restaurant. In my job, I am never in one place during the day. I use a cooler with blue ice packets to preserve and cool my food throughout the day to keep it fresh during any kind of weather. I can usually pack my lunch for less than a dollar a day. I do not know many places that you can go to buy lunch for a dollar.

Lunch Tip: Instead of using lunch meat, prepare tuna, chicken, or egg salad for lunches. Sliced cheese or peanut butter and jelly sandwiches are delicious and economical also.

Leftovers

When I was growing up, my mother never threw away leftovers. She was very creative in using the leftover food that she had in her refrigerator. We never kept anything over three or four days as a food safety precaution. After three days, it was usually thrown in the trash. I have taken the use of leftovers one step further in that I will freeze items that I cannot use in three days or less. The trick to keeping frozen foods fresh is properly storing them. I have included a list of foods that freeze well and some tips for their storage.

Items That Freeze Well

- Leftover pizza (Sometimes I will buy Pizza Hut pizza when they have a special and freeze one for another time. Often, many pizza restaurants will advertise a buy one get one free or half off. This purchase can be as cheap as buying frozen pizza from the supermarket. In addition, according to your personal taste preference, the pizza that you buy from the restaurant is better than frozen pizzas at the supermarket. My personal favorite is thick-crust Pizza Hut pizza. I don't eat it often because it has a lot of fats, but every once in a while, I will treat myself to the flavor that I love.)
- Baked Chicken
- Turkey and Dressing
- Beef Pot Roast
- Chili
- Soups (Bean and Split Pea)
- Homemade breads, muffins, and biscuits
- Cheesecake
- Cookies
- Cakes
- Soup Stock

How to Store and Use Leftovers

Some people prefer freshly prepared meals each night as opposed to leftovers. However, leftovers can save a tremendous amount of money over a period of a year. In addition, it gives the cook a night off during the week. The additional plus is that you are not incurring extra cost since you have already paid for the food when you prepared it the first time. Leftovers can be used in a variety of ways.

- Skip a day or two between using leftovers if you do not like to eat the same meal two nights in a row.
- Freeze leftovers for a family meal or in individual portions.

- Use individual frozen leftovers as a buffet. Each family member can select his/her favorite meal, and it can be heated in the microwave.

For two person working families, a good way to *share the load of planning and cooking dinner meals* for the family is for the husband and wife to take turns doing the cooking. Two teacher friends of mine with two growing sons would each share this responsibility. Whoever cooked the meal prepared enough for two nights. In this way, Monday through Thursday nights were covered, and Friday nights became the cooks' night off. On that night, the family would eat out at a local restaurant. This tradition helped to bring the family closer together over a good meal, and neither spouse felt the cooking burden was all his or hers to shoulder.

Recipes for Leftover Chicken

Baked chicken is a great meal to prepare on a Saturday or Sunday because you have more prep time than on weeknights. Usually, there will be leftovers after the family has eaten. With the following recipes, you do not need more than a cup or a cup and a half of meat. These dishes are called "meal stretchers." This type of cooking can have a significant impact on your family budget since meat is the most expensive item that we purchase in the grocery store.

Baked Chicken

One 3-5 lb chicken
salt and black pepper
olive oil
aluminum foil
roasting pan

- Remove the paper package inside the carcass of the chicken that contains the liver, gizzard, and neck.
- Rinse the inside of the chicken.
- Place the chicken in a roasting pan.
- Baste the chicken with olive oil.
- Wrap the tips of the wings and the ends of the legs with aluminum foil to keep them from getting burned.
- Sprinkle the chicken with desired amount of salt and black pepper.
- Place the top on the roasting pan.
- Place the chicken in the oven and bake at 375 degrees for the first 20 minutes and then turn the oven down to 350 degrees for the remainder of the baking time. Chicken is usually baked for 20 minutes per pound. Use a meat thermometer placed in the thicker breast part of the chicken to determine whether the meat is fully cooked. Chicken should be baked until the thermometer reads 190 degrees. Always bake fresh chicken to this temperature in order to kill any salmonella bacteria.

Stuffing for Chicken

8-12 slices of white bread
½ tsp poultry seasoning
½ tsp sage
½ tsp salt
½ tsp black pepper
½ tsp thyme
1 cup celery (diced)
1 cup onion (diced)
1 tbsp olive oil

Cut the bread into cubes by slicing in strips and then cutting across the strips. Use a serrated bread knife to cut the bread. Add seasonings to the bread cubes. Sauté the onion and celery in 1 tbsp of olive oil. Add the vegetables to the seasoned bread cubes. Mix ingredients well. Put stuffing in the cavity of the whole chicken and bake until inside temperature of the stuffing is 165 degrees.

Alternative: Spread the stuffing in the bottom of a greased casserole dish. Cover the top of the stuffing with 4 or 5 browned chicken parts. Bake at 350 degrees for 1 hour and 15 minutes.

Chicken Broth/Stock

- After you have used the chicken for your meal, debone the leftover chicken from your baked chicken.
- Refrigerate the meat.
- Throw all the bones and the carcass from the baked chicken into a pot.
- Add 3 cups of water.
- Bring to a boil and cook for one hour.
- Strain the broth from the chicken. Throw the bones and fat away.
- Reserve and refrigerate the chicken stock and use up to 3 days after cooking.
- Freeze the stock after 3 days for future use.
- Always label the outside of the package with a date and the name of the content.

Chicken Soup

By using the meat from the back of the chicken and the wings, you can prepare a soup that is fit for a king or queen. Use the following ingredients:

- Leftover chicken from back and wings
- 2 carrots
- 2 stalks of celery
- 2 chicken bouillon cubes
- 3 medium potatoes or ¼ cup of dry rice
- 1 quart of water or chicken stock

Begin by boiling the water and bouillon cubes. Peel and cut the carrots in half lengthwise and then slice. (This is a fast way to make the pieces smaller). Peel and cut the celery into small pieces. Add these ingredients to the boiling water. Peel and cut potatoes into small pieces and add to the water (You can replace the potatoes with 1/4 cup dried rice). Cook the soup until the potatoes and carrots are tender (approximately 25-30 minutes). Do not overcook. Add the chicken pieces the last 2 minutes so that you do not cook the flavor out of it.

Serve with a salad and fresh biscuits or muffins, and you have a very hearty nutritional meal.

Servings: 4
Cost: Approximately $1.00

Chow Mein (My Mother's Recipe)

chicken (1 to 2 cups of leftovers)
½ cup of onion
½ cup of celery
2 cups of unsalted chicken broth
1-2 tbsp of soy sauce
2-3 tbsp of cornstarch mixed with ¼ cup water
1 16-oz can of bean sprouts
1 8-oz can of water chestnuts
1 cup of dry rice (cooked in 2 cups of boiling water with 1 tsp salt)
2 cups of Rice Krispies (slightly browned in 1 tbsp olive oil)

- Sauté onion and celery in olive oil.
- Add chicken broth and heat to boiling.
- Add 1-2 cups cooked chicken.
- Thicken with cornstarch mixed with ¼ cup water.
- Add 1 to 2 tbsp soy sauce to this mixture.
- Add bean sprouts and water chestnuts last. (Do not overcook these items.)
- Serve over cooked rice.
- Brown (slightly) Rice Krispies in olive oil and serve with chow mien.
- You may also use chow mien noodles.

Servings: 4-6
Cost: Approximately $3.50

Chicken Stew

1-2 cups of leftover chicken
2 cups of chicken broth or gravy
1-2 chicken bouillon cubes
3-4 medium potatoes (cut into pieces)
3 carrots (cut in slices)
2 stalks of celery (diced)
1 medium onion (diced)
¼ cup of water mixed with 3 tbsp cornstarch
1 cup of frozen peas
1 cup of frozen corn

Start with leftover chicken (1-2 cups). Cut the meat into small pieces. Put chicken broth and gravy into a saucepan and bring to a boil. Add a chicken bouillon cube to add extra flavor. Add potatoes (yellow potatoes have the best flavor) and carrots. Add diced celery and onion. Cook the potatoes, carrots, celery, and onion until tender. Thicken the broth and vegetables with cornstarch and water. Add the frozen peas and corn the last 5 minutes of cooking so that these vegetables remain crisp. Add the leftover chicken last, and just heat 1 or 2 more minutes.

Servings: 4-6
Cost: Approximately $3.00

Chicken Potpie

- Use the same recipe for chicken stew.
- Pour the stew into a 10" by 13" baking dish.
- Make the crust by using the recipe for biscuits (p. 69).
- Roll out the biscuit between 2 pieces of wax paper.
- Roll the biscuit dough big enough to cover the 10" by 13" dish.
- Bake in the oven at 400 degrees until the biscuit is browned for approximately 15-20 minutes.

Note: You can prepare several smaller dishes of this recipe and then freeze them for nights that you don't want to cook. Reheat at 350 degrees until heated through.

Chicken à la King

2 cups of chicken broth
2 chicken bouillon cubes
2 cups of chicken
1 cup of frozen peas
1 cup of diced celery (sauté)
cornstarch to thicken
3 cups of cooked rice

- Sauté the celery in a small Teflon pan.
- Bring 2 cups of chicken broth to a rolling boil.
- Remove the broth from heat.
- Mix 2 tbsp of cornstarch with ¼ cup of water.
- Add the cornstarch mixture to the slightly cooled chicken broth.
- Mix until well blended. Bring this mixture to a boil again, stirring constantly until thickened.
- Add the chicken and frozen peas and cook until the peas are heated.
- Serve the chicken à la king over cooked rice.

Crock-Pot Meals for Working Families

When I was a principal of an elementary school, I had several young assistant principals who had young children to feed at home after work. I developed these Crock-Pot recipes to give to my young assistants to help them in having a healthy meal prepared when they arrived home. When parents work all day, it is still important for them to prepare good, healthy, and tasty meals for their families. Use these do-ahead Crock-Pot meals to have everything ready when your family arrives home after work, school, and after-school activities. The trade-off is that you will have to get up 20-30 minutes earlier in the morning in order to do this food prep, but your long-term savings and food nutrition are well worth the extra effort early in the morning.

Pork and Vegetable Medley

1 lb boneless pork chops	1 cup of sliced carrots
1 lb can of diced tomatoes	2 stalks of celery
2 tbsp of brown sugar or molasses	1 small onion
1 tbsp of Worcestershire sauce	1 T of vinegar

Slice pork chops into strips. Brown the pork in a Teflon pan with no oil. Put the pork and all the remaining ingredients in a Crock-Pot. Stir and cook 8-10 hours on low. Serve with cooked white or brown rice. You may cook the rice in the morning or the night before. Refrigerate it and reheat in microwave when you get home from work.

Chicken or Pork with Cream Sauce

1 can cream of chicken soup or cream of mushroom soup
1 cup of water
2 tsp of Worchester sauce
1 to 2 lb boneless/skinless chicken breasts or tenders
1 to 2 lb boneless/skinless pork

- Heat 1 cup of water to boiling.
- Add 1 can of soup and Worchester sauce.
- Mix with a wire whisk until smooth.
- Brown meat in a nonstick skillet.
- Layer chicken or pork in Crock-Pot with the soup mixture.
- Cook 8 to 10 hours on low.
- Serve with rice.

Baked Chicken or Chuck Roast and Vegetables

1 chicken
1 onion
2 stalks of celery cut up into pieces
5 medium potatoes
3 to 4 carrots or enough baby carrots for your family
1 chicken bouillon cube dissolved in 1 cup of boiling water (chicken)
1 beef bouillon cube dissolved in 1 cup of boiling water (beef roast)
Use a West Bend or other similar model of slow roaster.
Put a chicken or chuck roast in the slow roaster.
Add potatoes and carrots around the chicken or roast.
Sprinkle celery and onion on vegetables and chicken or roast.
Sprinkle salt, pepper, and a little thyme on top.
Cook for 8-10 hours on low.
Lipton's Onion soup mix is excellent sprinkled on top of the beef roast.

Beef and Noodles

round steak or beef leftovers
2 cans of cream of mushroom soup
1 can of water
1 beef bouillon cube
1 tbsp of Worchester sauce
egg noodles

Boil ½ can of water. Add bouillon cube until dissolved. Add soup and Worchester sauce. Stir with a wire whisk until smooth. Add the other ½ can of water. Cut round steak into strips and brown. Or use leftover beef cut into pieces or sliced. Layer the beef and soup mixture in a Crock-Pot. Cook all day on low. Before serving, cook the egg noodles according to the package directions. Serve the prepared beef casserole over cooked noodles.

Peppered Steak

1 lb round steak (cut into strips)
1 6-oz can of tomato paste
1 lb can of diced tomatoes
2 tbsp of Worchester sauce
1/2 cup of water
1 beef bouillon cube
1 green pepper (sliced into strips)
1 large onion (sliced)
3-4 cups of cooked rice

Dissolve beef bouillon cube in 1/4 cup of boiling water. Add all ingredients into Crock-Pot and cook 8-10 hours on low. Serve over rice. (This recipe is a great meal for company on a Friday night because it cooks while you are at work. The amount of ingredients can be doubled to serve 10-16 people).

Bean Soup

1 lb of dried navy beans
2 quarts of water
2 beef bouillon cubes
1/2 lb of sliced deli ham cut up small (optional)
2 carrots (shredded)
2 onions (diced)
1 lb can of diced tomatoes
1 6-oz can of tomato paste

Bring all ingredients to a boil. Cook in a pot on the stove for 2 to 3 hours. When the beans are tender, put the soup in a Crock-Pot to cook for another 8-10 hours.

Note: This dish is a great meal for a Saturday because you have extra time in the morning to soak and precook the dried beans.

Italian Pork Chops

1 can of Italian diced tomatoes
1 onion (sliced)
1 stalk of celery (diced)
4 boneless, skinless pork chops (browned)
2 tbsp of Worchester sauce
¼ cup of brown sugar

Prepare all the ingredients and place in a Crock-Pot. Cook for 8 to 10 hours during the day. Serve with rice or noodles.

Stuffed Ham Casserole (See Stuffed Ham Recipe)

7 medium/large white or yellow potatoes (sliced)
1 lb of stuffed ham with stuffing
2 onions (sliced)
2 cans of cream of mushroom soup

Boil 2 cups of water. Add soup and stir until smooth.

Layer the ingredients in the following order: soup, potatoes, onions, ham, soup, potatoes, onions, ham. Repeat this sequence as ingredients remain. This recipe tastes especially good using stuffed ham. This casserole has become many of our friends' favorite dish at an annual New Year's Eve party that we attend each year.

Stuffed Ham Soup (My original recipe)

2 quarts of stuffed ham broth (saved from boiling the stuffed ham)
2 cups of carrots cut in small pieces
3 cups of potatoes cut in small pieces
2 stalks of celery cut in small pieces
1 large onion (diced)
2 beef bouillon cubes
1 cup of leftover stuffed ham and stuffing (Recipe on p. 82)
2 cans of Campbell's Bean with Bacon Soup

Bring ham broth to a boil. Prepare the vegetables. Combine and cook all ingredients except the leftover ham and Campbell's Bean with Bacon Soup. Add these at the very end of the cooking when the vegetables are tender.

Crock-Pots and Entertaining

Over the years, I have entertained frequently for large numbers of people. I have held baby and wedding showers, wedding rehearsal dinners, family gatherings, Christmas parties, and school faculty beginning—and end-of-the-year parties for anywhere between twenty-five to one hundred guests. I have found that if you can prepare some meals or side dishes a few days ahead of time or even just a few hours ahead of time, Crock-Pots act as excellent containers to reheat or keep dishes warm from two to ten hours prior to when your guests arrive and your party begins. Some dishes that lend themselves well to using a Crock-Pot are the following:

- Hot apple cider
- Warm mulled wine
- Scalloped potatoes
- Soups
- Stews
- Peppered steak
- Stuffed ham and potato casserole
- Tangy barbecue meatballs (appetizer)
- Chili
- Cooked rice
- Pot roast
- Baked chicken
- Candied carrots

Economical Appetizers

Tuna Pâté

1 pkg cream cheese (softened)
1 can of white tuna
salt and pepper to taste
2 tbsp of minced dried onion

Mix all ingredients together with a fork and refrigerate until you are ready to serve. Serve tuna pâté with Nabisco Triscuit or Keebler Town House crackers.

Note: Before identifying this appetizer, many of my guests have thought this was a crab dip.

Chicken Salad Cracker Spread

1 16-oz canned chicken or turkey breast meat
¼ cup or 1 stalk of finely diced celery
¼ cup of Vidalia onion salad dressing

Dice celery finely. Flake the chicken in a bowl with a fork. Mix the salad dressing, celery, and chicken. Put in a fancy dish and refrigerate until your guests arrive. Serve with a variety of crackers. This appetizer has been a hit at my parties, and it has the advantage of being low fat for guests who like to watch their calories and fat intake.

Tangy Barbecued Meatballs

3 lbs of lean ground beef
3 tbsp of dried flaked onion
1 tsp of salt
1 tsp of black pepper
2 cups of grape jelly or jam
2 cups of barbecue sauce

Mix ground beef with flaked onion, salt, and black pepper. Roll beef mixture into 1 ½ inch balls. Brown/cook in a frying pan. Pour off any grease or liquid from the meatballs. In a separate pan, heat grape jelly or jam with the barbecue sauce until the jelly melts and mixes well with the barbecue sauce. Pour this mixture over the meatballs in the frying pan. When meatballs and sauce are bubbly, transfer to a Crock-Pot and keep warm until your party begins. Prepare several hours before your party.

Breads and Breakfast Foods

Basic Biscuit Recipe

2 cups of unbleached flour
2 tbsp sugar
3 tsp of baking powder
1 tsp of salt
1/3 cup of canola oil
2/3 cup of milk

- Measure all dry ingredients into a large bowl.
- Measure oil and milk into a smaller mixing bowl.
- Pour the liquid ingredients into the dry mixture.
- Using a wooden spoon, stir until the flour mixture is just moistened (Do not beat this). Without touching the dough, spoon it onto a 12" by 16" piece of wax paper. Using the wax paper, knead the dough 10 to 15 times by folding the dough in half and then pressing down. Continue this using the wax paper and not your hands. (The warmth from your bare hands will have a negative effect on the texture of the biscuit.)

Roll the dough between two pieces of wax paper to ½- to 5/8-inch thickness. Cut the biscuits with a 2-inch biscuit cutter. Bake the biscuits in the oven at 425 degrees for 9 minutes or until lightly browned.

This recipe is very economical, and it can afford you to serve fresh bread every night of the week. We have a family tradition of breaking out the jam after dinner to have on one more biscuit as we top off our dinner. Many of our sons' friends over the years have joined us in this tradition as they have enjoyed "Mrs. Brown's" homemade biscuits.

Biscuit Variations

Bacon Egg and Cheese Biscuits

Bake biscuits as directed above. Split the biscuit and add a fried hard egg, 2 slices of fried bacon, and a slice of American cheese. This sandwich tastes as good as any breakfast sandwich that you can purchase at a fast-food chain.

Biscuit Variation for Strawberry Shortcake

Add 1/4 cup of sugar instead of the 2 tablespoons of sugar in the basic biscuit recipe. Roll the dough thinner and cut with a 3-inch biscuit cutter. Bake the same as above. Remove from the oven and split in half. Placing the cut sides down on a dessert plate, scoop vanilla ice cream on top of the biscuit and add strawberries or any other fresh fruit that you might like such as peaches, blueberries, or blackberries.

Scones

Scones are nothing more than a biscuit with a variety of different fruits or flavorings to make different recipes.

Using my basic biscuit recipe above, you can make a number of flavor variations. These are some ingredients you can add to the biscuit recipe right before kneading:

- ½ cup of raisins
- ½ cup of mini chocolate chips
- ½ cup of grated cheddar cheese

Roll the dough into a circle and cut into 8 pie wedge shapes. Bake on a cookie sheet until brown for approximately 15 to 20 minutes at 425 degrees.

Pizza (Homemade Dough)

Put in a mixing bowl 1 cup of warm water and 1 pkg of yeast.
Let this mixture stand for 5 minutes and then stir.
Add to this liquid mixture the following ingredients and then mix well:

- 1 tsp of sugar
- 1 tsp of salt
- 1 tbsp of shortening

Next, measure the following dry ingredient into the liquid mixture:

- 1 ½ cups all purpose flour

Beat until smooth.

Add about 1 more cup of flour using enough to make the dough just barely firm enough to handle. You may need a little more than the one cup.

After mixing these ingredients, you will knead the dough for five minutes until it becomes elastic.

Do this by flouring a cutting board and then folding the dough in half, then pressing down, turning the dough a quarter turn, and then folding again and then pressing it down. There is an art to kneading dough, and it is an important part of the process of making pizza dough or any bread dough that requires yeast. Kneading the dough ensures that the yeast will be worked into the bread, and this helps it to rise.

Grease a 15" pizza pan. Place the dough in the middle of the pan. Press the center of the dough with the palm of your hand. Turn the pan one-quarter turn and continue to press with the palm of your hand. Continue this process until you have spread the dough to the outside edges of the pan. Cover the pan with a clean dish towel and let rise for 15 minutes, longer if you want thicker crust.

Before spreading your toppings, brush the dough with olive oil. Sprinkle with Parmesan cheese. Add the pizza sauce and then top with your favorites pizza toppings (Perkins 1965).

Pancakes from Scratch

Ingredients	4-5 cakes	8-10 cakes	13-15 cakes
flour	1 cup	2 cups	3 cups
sugar	1 tbsp	2 tbsp	3 tbsp
baking powder	2 tsp	4 tsp	2 tbsp
salt	½ tsp	1 tsp	1 ½ tsp
egg	1	2	3
melted utter	1 tbsp	2 tbsp	3 tbsp
milk	½ cup + 2 tbsp	1 cup + ¼ cup	1½ cup + 6 tbsp
vanilla	½ tsp	1 tsp	1½ tsp

Mix together the dry ingredients. Add milk, egg, melted butter, and vanilla all at one time. Mix the batter enough to blend the dry ingredients with the liquids. Add the additional milk to the batter. The batter should not be beaten and should contain some lumps.

Using a large tablespoon or a ¼ measuring cup, pour the batter into a hot griddle (medium heat). Higher heat will burn the pancakes. Wait until bubbles form on the top of the pancake and begin to pop before you turn the pancake. Check the bottom of the pancake to make sure they are brown before taking them out of the pan.

Muffins

Put into a large mixing bowl:

2 cups of flour minus 2 tablespoons
2 tbsp of sugar (or up to 1/2 cup of sugar)
1 tbsp of baking powder
½ tsp of salt

Mix in another bowl:

1 egg (slightly beaten)
1 cup of milk
¼ cup of melted butter

Pour liquid mixture over the flour mixture. Stir only enough to dampen the flour. Spoon mixture into buttered muffin tins (Or spray PAM into muffin pan). Fill the tins about 2/3 full. Bake at 400 degrees about 15-18 minutes until browned on top. Makes 12 muffins (Perkins 1965).

Blueberry Muffins

Reserve 2 tbsp of flour from the original mixture. Sprinkle the flour over 1 cup of blueberries. Stir the blueberries into the batter last. (Use 2 tbsp less than a half of a cup of sugar in this recipe.)

Cheese Muffins

Add 1 cup of grated cheddar cheese to the batter.

Bacon Muffins

Cook ¼ lb of bacon cooked in the microwave.
Reserve 1 tbsp of bacon grease from the cooked bacon and add it to the batter.

Favorite Coffee Cake

1 ½ cups of all-purpose flour
¾ cup of granulated sugar
2 ½ tsp of baking powder
¾ tsp of salt
¼ cup of shortening
¾ cup of milk
1 egg

Measure all the ingredients into a large bowl. Stir all the ingredients until moistened. Beat for ½ minute. Pour ½ of the batter in a greased and floured nine-inch round pan or eight-inch square pan. Sprinkle ½ of the streusel topping on this half of the batter. Pour the remaining batter on top and carefully spread it to cover the streusel. Sprinkle the remainder of the streusel on top. Bake at 350 degrees for 30-35 minutes or until a toothpick inserted in the cake comes out clean (General Mills, Inc.1969).

Streusel-filled Topping

Mix ½ cup brown sugar, 2 tsp cinnamon, ½ cup finely chopped walnuts and 2 tbsp melted butter.

Note: This recipe is a family favorite. My son, Randy, frequently requests me to bake this coffee cake.

Casseroles and Stews as Meal Stretchers

Cat Creek Quiche

This recipe was shared with me in the early 1980s by my friend and financial advisor, Eric Bargar. It has been used well over two hundred times.

1½ cups of milk
3 eggs
dash of red pepper
dash of nutmeg
½ stick of butter or margarine
½ cup of Bisquick
1 small onion

Put all above ingredients into a blender for about 30 seconds until onion is chopped up. Spray PAM inside a glass pie plate. Pour blender egg mixture into the dish. First add the cheese you want (about 1 cup). Then add a cup of your favorite topping.

Topping Combinations:

broccoli and sharp cheese
spinach and mozzarella
sausage (cooked and drained) and mozzarella
crab and a little shredded Swiss cheese and mozzarella
can of tuna (drained) and sharp cheese
bacon and cheddar cheese
broccoli and cauliflower and sharp cheese
turkey or chicken and sharp cheese

Beef Recipes

Meatballs and Noodles

1 can tomato soup
½ can of water
2 tsp minced onions
½ tsp thyme

Add these ingredients in a saucepan to begin simmering.

Mix 1 lb of ground beef with ½ tsp garlic salt, ½ tsp thyme, ¼ tsp black pepper and 1 tbsp parsley.

Brown meatballs and add to the tomato mixture.

Simmer for 30 minutes.

Cook noodles as directed and serve sauce and meatballs over the noodles.

Lasagna

1 lb of sausage, browned
1 lb of ground beef, browned
1 tsp of salt
1 clove of garlic
1 tbsp of basil
1 lb can of diced tomatoes
1 lb can of tomato sauce
1 6-oz can of tomato paste

Mix all of this and simmer for 30-45 minutes. Prego spaghetti sauce can be used as a substitute for this part of the recipe.

Mix 3 cups of ricotta or cottage cheese, 2 tbsp of parsley, ½ cup of Parmesan cheese, ½ tsp of pepper, and 2 eggs beaten. Set aside. Cook 1 lb of pasta for lasagna.

Layer the tomato and meat mixture, pasta, and cheese mixture beginning and ending with tomato mixture. Bake at 375 degrees for 45-60 minutes. Sprinkle Parmesan cheese on the top of the lasagna during the last 10 minutes of baking (General Mills 1969, 312).

Hamburger Bean Bake (Esther Brown)

2 lb of ground beef (browned)
1 cup of brown sugar
1 cup of ketchup
1 pkg of Lipton Onion Soup Mix
1 46-oz can of kidney beans
1 32-oz can of baked beans

Mix all ingredients together and bake at 350 degrees for 45 minutes in a 4-quart baking dish or put in Crock-Pot and heat until bubbly (2 hours).

Chili

This recipe was handed down to me by my mother, Cecilia Hayden. This dish is an excellent crowd-pleaser and can be prepared the day before and then put into the Crock-Pot to reheat 2-3 hours before a party or family gathering.

1 large onion (halved and then sliced)
1 green pepper (diced)
1 lb ground beef
1 8-oz can tomato paste
1 28-oz can diced tomatoes
1 16-oz can of tomato sauce
¼ cup vinegar
3-4 tsp chili powder

Brown the hamburger. Add onion and green pepper. Sauté these vegetables with the hamburger for about 5 minutes. Drain grease. Put the hamburger and vegetables in a large Dutch kettle. Add tomato paste, tomato sauce, and diced tomatoes. Add vinegar and chili powder. Simmer for 1 to 2 hours. Add kidney bean and continue to heat until kidney beans are hot.

Shepherd's Pie

1 lb ground beef
1 can tomato soup
1 10-oz pkg frozen string beans
3-4 carrots (peeled and sliced)
1 medium onion (chopped)
2 lb mashed potatoes (You may use instant potatoes if you are short on time)
½ cup grated sharp cheddar cheese (optional)

Brown ground beef and onion together until ground beef is cooked through. Cook green beans for 5 minutes. Peel and cook potatoes. Peel, slice, and cook carrots (cook for 20 minutes). Mash potatoes when they are finished cooking. Cook green beans and carrots (do not overcook). Add these two vegetables as well as the can of tomato soup into browned ground beef and onion mixture. Fold the beef mixture and vegetables together. Put this mixture on the bottom of a greased 10 by 13 inch baking dish. Spoon mashed potatoes around the edge of the dish. Cook at 350 degrees for 30 minutes. Add grated cheddar cheese the last 5 minutes of baking.

Meat Loaf

1 lb ground beef
2 medium onions (chopped)
¼ cup green pepper (chopped)
½ cup dried oatmeal
1 egg
¼ cup ketchup
1 tsp salt
1 tsp black pepper
5 medium potatoes (peeled and halved)
4 carrots (peeled and cut in half and then lengthwise into strips)
1 lb can of diced tomatoes

Mix the first set of ingredients and one of the chopped onions and form this mixture into a loaf. Place the meat loaf into a Teflon frying pan. Place the peeled potatoes and carrots around the meat loaf. Sprinkle the second chopped onion on top of the potatoes, carrots, and meat loaf. Pour the diced tomatoes on top of the potatoes, carrots, and meat loaf. Sprinkle with a little extra salt and black pepper. Cook for 1 to 1 ½ hours or until carrots and potatoes are cooked.

Serves 4-6

<u>Southern Maryland Stuffed Ham</u> (Brown's Version)

22-25 lb corned ham
10 lbs of cabbage
4-5 lbs kale
2-3 lbs onions
1 bunch of celery
Cheese cloth
salt
black pepper
red pepper (ground and flaked)

Cabbage. Wash, quarter, and core. Cut into smaller pieces. Use a blender and fill with water. Add cabbage and chop using the pulse button. Be careful not to grind the cabbage into mush. Drain the water and put this in a large pan.

Kale. Wash. Pull the stems off the kale. Use a food processor to chop kale. Put it into the top of the processor. Use the blade that slices. This will cut it the way you want it. Add this to the cabbage in the pan.

Put approximately 3 cups of water into the pan. Bring to boil and stir frequently. Boil for only about 3 minutes, enough to cook down the kale and cabbage slightly. Drain reserving the juice for your pan to cook the ham.

Celery. Peel skin off outside of celery. Wash and cut in small pieces for food processor. Chop celery in food processor. Be careful not to cut it into mush.

Onion. Peel onions and use food processor to chop onion. Add celery and onion to cabbage and kale mixture, which has been drained and has been placed in a large pan for mixing. Do not cook onion and celery. Add spices (salt and pepper to your liking, we like it *hot, hot, hot*). Make holes in the ham with a long knife being careful not to come through the opposite end. Stuff the ham with your vegetable mixture using your fingers. Always keep the ham on a cookie sheet as many juices will be made. Change the cookie sheet several times during the process of stuffing. Always reserve the juice for the water in your big pan to cook the ham. When finished stuffing, wrap the ham with cheesecloth and tie it tight. Cook ham outside on a cooker with water filled to 1 inch above the ham. Cook until a meat thermometer registers 160 degrees (Approximately 20 minutes per pound).

Notes: Place ham fat side up or it will be dry. Watch carefully toward the end of the cooking because from 150 degrees onward, the ham cooks very quickly to 160 degrees. If you overcook the ham, the meat will be dry. *Do not leave the ham in the water once it reaches 160 degrees; otherwise, it will keep cooking.* Cool and keep in the refrigerator. If it is cold outside especially at night, put it on a cookie sheet, and place it inside your grill. It will cool much quicker than in your refrigerator. Cover ham with saran wrap when putting it into refrigerator or it will smell everything else in your fridge. I have used a white plastic garbage bag and tied it with the metal ties provided. Do not use aluminum foil directly on the ham as it will turn it a green color and give it a metal taste.

Using your Freezer to Preserve Freshness

Whenever I freeze food items, I double bag them for freshness and to prevent freezer burn. You should buy Ziploc bags from a wholesale warehouse since they are about half the price as a regular supermarket. If your item already has an outside wrapping such as the wrapping on a loaf of bread, put it in a Ziploc bag or plastic container such as Rubbermaid.

You should always freeze leftovers even if it is only enough for one or two servings. When you combine a number of these, your whole family can eat for dinner and have a choice of what they want for that night. Just defrost and reheat the item in the microwave. You will have quick meals with very little fuss. Leftovers can be frozen on Styrofoam plates or glassware that can go from freezer to oven. If you use Styrofoam to freeze your food, transfer it to a microwavable plate for reheating and serving.

Directions for Freezing a Variety of Food Items

Leftovers. Cover the top of your prepared food dish with plastic wrap. Then place the wrapped container in a Ziploc bag for a second wrap.

Cookies. Use a Christmas tin to store cookies. Layer the cookies with a piece of wax paper between each layer. Before putting the lid on top of the can, place a piece of saran wrap on the top of the can. Place the whole can in a gallon Ziploc bag. The trick is to use tin containers small enough to fit in your gallon-sized Ziploc bags. Cookies will stay fresh up to 3-6 months by double bagging them.

Juices and Broth from Meats. Store these liquids in a plastic container such as Rubbermaid or Glad containers and then place the plastic container in a one- or two-gallon Ziploc bag.

Bread. Put the loaf of bread in a gallon Ziploc bag. Then place two individually bagged loaves of bread in a two-gallon Ziploc bag.

Butter. Keep butter in original packaging. Put in a one-quart Ziploc bag.

Ice Cream. Using a two-gallon Ziploc bag, you can store two half gallon containers of ice cream.

Note: Ziploc bags and Glad storage containers can be recycled and used again. Rinse your Ziploc bag and dry by placing a drinking glass on a dishtowel with the bag over top of the glass. Do not remove until the bag is dry.

Tricks to Lighten Your Fat Intake

After roasting meats such as chicken and beef, the bottom of the pan is filled with rich juices and fats from the meat. In order to reduce your fats and still use these juices, use this trick:

- Drain the fats and juices into a glass container.
- Let it sit for five minutes.
- Pour the liquid into another glass container.
- Place a cup or so of ice cubes in the liquid.
- When the liquid is cold, the grease should harden at this point.
- Skim off the hardened grease.
- You are ready to use the rich juices as a soup stock or in your gravies.

Olive oil is a much-healthier fat to use in cooking, and it adds to your good cholesterol count. Use olive oil in the following ways:

- Stir frying vegetables
- Frying eggs
- Grilled cheese sandwiches by brushing on olive oil and browning the sandwich in a Teflon pan

When baking cakes or making biscuits, you can substitute canola oil in your recipe in place of vegetable oil. Canola oil does not have the strong flavor that olive oil does. In particular, use canola oil in your biscuit recipe and when a cake mix calls for vegetable oil.

Places to Shop for Food and Household Items

In each community or neighborhood, grocery stores or supermarkets can be found that carry food products at a significantly lower price when compared to others in the same area. A good way to investigate this is to choose twenty items such as milk, bread, cereal, mayonnaise, detergent, etc., and then go to five area markets choosing ones that you think are the cheapest. Gather the prices of each item and use the worksheet provided in the template. When you are finished, add the list of twenty items from the one store. Do this for each list. When you are finished, you will have a comparison between five stores of the overall cost for those twenty items. For fun, choose one store that you know is high and include it in your worksheet (See appendix A).

Toiletries are best purchased in bulk at wholesale warehouses such as Sam's Club, Costco's, or BJ's. If you are a smaller family, shopping for your hair, skin, and other health and beauty products are best purchased at a Wal-Mart. You can find items significantly cheaper by as much as 25 to 50 percent less.

Comparison Shopping

Each week, local newspapers carry area grocers' weekly sales flyers. Pick two or three stores based on your own assessment of which ones are the cheapest in your area. These ads usually come out on Wednesdays, and prices reflected are either from Wednesday to Sunday or Sunday to Saturday. You will have to read the top or bottom of the flyer carefully to determine when the ad runs in each store. Spend fifteen minutes perusing them and finding the best values for each store. Often, you may have the same item in three different newspapers at three different prices.

It takes a little more time, but shopping at two or three stores rather than one will yield your family greater savings at the end of the month and ultimately at the end of the year.

I have a rule of thumb. I never buy anything unless it is on sale or I have a coupon for the item. A purchase using a coupon added to a sale item can be a real value for you—the consumer. You often hear people interviewed on television who have bought an item for just pennies or nothing by using coupons on an already discounted item.

I have taken three ads, and I will call them market A, B, and C. I went through these ads and have pulled the sale items to show you the comparisons for the same item advertised in each of the three stores during the same period of time. (See appendix C for additional worksheet).

Item	Market A	Market B	Market C
cantaloupe	2.99 lb		Buy 1, Get 1 Free
grapes		0.99 lb	1.79 lb
golden apples		1.49 lb	
18 oz peanut butter		2.50	
roasting chicken	0.99 lb	1.29 lb	
chicken leg quarters	0.99 lb		0.47 lb
ice cream	2.50 half gallon	1.99 half gallon	2.79 half gallon
lean ground beef	3.99 lb	2.49 lb	2.79 lb
pork chops	2.99 lb	2.49 lb	
country style pork	2.49 lb		1.79 lb
salmon fillets	5.99 lb		6.99 lb
pork tenderloin	1.99 lb		3.99 lb

Comparison of Twenty-Five Items
(not on sale) at Three Supermarkets

In addition, I have visited three major supermarkets and did a comparison of commonly used products to determine the price of each item (not on sale) on one particular day. These items were not on sale, and they were researched on August 30, 2008. It is interesting to look at the differences in prices in each store. In addition, one market has significantly different totals when compared to the other two.

Items	Market A	Market B	Market C
eggs (dozen, store brand)	2.19	1.33	1.63
milk (skim, gallon)	3.99	3.99	3.40
milk (2% of a gallon)	3.99	3.99	3.40
Kraft (12 oz of sliced cheese)	3.69	2.99	2.98
Gold Medal flour (5 lb)	2.99	2.59	2.52
Kellogg cornflakes (18 oz)	3.49	4.00	2.58
General Mills Cheerios (14 oz)	3.49	4.05	2.78
Sunbeam bread (22 oz)	2.79	2.69	1.50
Jell-O (gelatin)	1.00	0.79	0.50
Jell-O (pudding)	0.99	0.89	0.82
lunch meat Oscar Mayer (9 oz deli)	4.19	3.99	2.98
Hellman's mayonnaise (32 oz)	4.29	4.79	2.87
Kraft salad dressing (16 oz)	3.29	2.79	1.58
Iceberg lettuce	1.59	1.19	1.44
celery	1.99	1.29	1.48
potatoes (white)	2.99 (3 lb)	3.99 (5 lb)	3.50 (10 lb)
apples (delicious)	4.99 (3 lb)	5.99 (3 lb)	5.68 (8 lb)
Breakstone sour cream (16 oz)	2.29	2.09	1.62
whole chicken (Purdue)	1.69 lb	1.49 lb	0.78 lb
Minute Maid orange juice (½ gal)	2.99	3.49	2.73
Philadelphia cream cheese (8 oz)	2.29	2.19	1.63
Jif peanut butter (28 oz)	3.99	4.25	2.98
Total	65.19	64.85	51.38
Difference (Highest to lowest=$13.77)			

Shopping for Food Products

Penny-wise, pound-foolish

-Edward Topsell

Coupons (Using and Managing)

Clipping coupons can be fun for the family and a challenging way to save money. Sunday mornings or afternoons can be used as a time to gather around the newspaper to find and clip coupons together. An *added benefit* is that your child will be reading, talking about money/math, and learning a life skill about saving money and being thrifty. Your child may pick out an item that you do not typically buy thereby encouraging him to try something new to eat in the house.

You can obtain coupons in the Sunday newspaper, in magazines, and often online. There are several ways to organize coupons. Without an organizer, you will eventually stop using them because it will be too much to go through a pile of coupons to find the right one.

I use a *plastic check organizer* or *expandable case* to organize my coupons. You should label the file in an alphabetical fashion and include major categories. Here are the categories that I use. (Preprinted labels can be found in appendix E.)

- Baking Needs
- Beverages
- Bread and Crackers
- Cleaning products
- Condiments
- Dairy
- Fruits
- Meats
- Miscellaneous
- Paper products
- Snacks
- Toiletries
- Vegetables

Expiration dates are important to watch. As you organize your coupons, you may want to put coupons that will expire within two to four weeks in the front of each section.

Purchasing Meat

Chicken

When purchasing chicken, *buy whole chickens* if you want your food dollar to stretch even further. Typically, at large wholesale stores such as Sam's Club, BJ's, and Costco, chickens will cost around $0.69 to $0.79 a pound. Chickens are usually sold with two in a package. Cut up the chickens and store the pieces in Ziploc bags in the freezer. Again, double bag your meat to avoid freezer burn and preserve freshness. You may package the chicken in a variety of ways for future use.

Two Whole Chickens Yield the Following Meals

Feeding a family of four on two whole chickens

Amounts in Each Package	Serves	Uses
4 chicken breasts	4-6	Serve whole breast to adults and cut breasts in half for children.
4 legs	4	Bake using barbecue sauce, seasoned salt, or corn flakes.
4 thighs	4	Bake, barbecue sauce, seasoned salt, or cornflakes.
2 chicken backs	4	Boil in 3 cups of water and pick off meat for soup. Use the broth for your soup and add desired vegetables.
4 wings	2	Cut up and discard the tip of the wing. Make appetizers.

Feeding a family of two on one whole chicken

Amounts in Each Package	Serves	Uses
1 whole chicken (uncut)	2-3 meals	Bake whole chicken. Use leftovers for one to two more meals.
2 legs	2	Bake, barbecue sauce, seasoned salt, or cornflakes.
2 thighs	2	Bake, barbecue sauce, seasoned salt, or cornflakes.
1 chicken back	2	Boil in 3 cups of water and pick off meat for soup. Use the broth for your soup and add desired vegetables.
2 wings	2	Cut up and discard the tip of the wing. Make appetizers.

For approximately 6 to 7 dollars, you can feed a family of four for $1.75 a day for four days.

Beef

Consumers in our country eat a lot more meat than is necessary for healthy living. A three-ounce serving (the size of your fist) is plenty for a serving. To make your meat budget, which is the most costly purchase on your supermarket list, extend even further, use ground beef for many recipes. Ground beef can be a dollar stretcher as well as a meal stretcher.

Amount in Each Package	Serves	Uses
½ to ¾ pounds of ground beef	4-6	chili, spaghetti, soups, lasagna, meatballs, meat loaf

Grocery Lists

A grocery list can help you avoid the temptation of buying impulsively when you arrive at the supermarket. Keep an *ongoing list of items* that you run out of in your kitchen for cooking or everyday living household items. This practice *helps you to avoid making a separate trip to the store for just a few items.* Some people use a magnetic tablet/list that they attach to their refrigerator. This practice helps you to reduce the amount of unnecessary buying that you do when you get into the store.

When going grocery shopping, make sure that you are not hungry because this can increase the amount of unnecessary buying that you do.

Make a menu for the week or even the month and then outline each of the items that you will need to make the meals. Check your pantry, refrigerator, and freezer to make sure that you have everything that you need. If you don't have an item, immediately put it on the list so you don't forget it when it is time to shop. In addition, planning meals for the month can help you to determine which items that you can buy in bulk at your closest warehouse store.

Use the convenient pantry list in appendix D to help you keep a running list of market needs.

Buddy Shopping

When I was growing up in the 1950s, my mother would always bring along a friend as she did the grocery shopping on Thursday nights. This outing was fun for all who came along, and it also saved gas money for the other person who came.

In today's markets, we have many wholesale establishments that sell their products in bulk. Two people from two different families who have either smaller families or just a husband and wife in the household can buy items and split the packages or contents to save money. Some items that work well for splitting are:

- rice (10 lb)
- sugar (10 lb)
- flour (10 lb)
- nuts (3 lb)
- meats (5+ lb)
- tuna (8 in a package)
- lunch meat (comes in 2 or 3 1-lb packages)
- sliced American cheese (comes in 3-lb packages)
- eggs (2 1-dozen packages)
- bacon (3 1-lb packages)
- frozen chicken (usually comes in a 4-5-lb bag)
- whole fresh chickens (2 in a bag)
- hot dogs (2 or 3 1-lb packages)
- graham crackers (6 packages)
- vanilla wafers (2 packages)
- macaroni and cheese (6 boxes)
- bottled water (24-35 bottles)
- dishwashing detergent (4 lb)
- laundry detergent (250 oz)

- Windex (128 oz)
- paper towels (12-24 rolls)
- toilet paper (24 rolls)
- toothpaste (2-3 in a package)
- comet (4 in a package)
- breakfast bars/rice crispy treats (24-36 in a box)
- bread (2 loaves in a package)
- peanut butter (2 jars in a package)
- jelly (2 to 3 jars in a package)
- olive oil (1 gallon bottle)
- fresh vegetables (3+ lb)
- fresh fruits (5-lb bags)
- potatoes (10- or 20-lb bags)
- romaine lettuce (5 heads)

Additional Ways to Preserve Food

On the Web site www.dollarstretcher.com, Irene Helen Zundel offers the following tips from her grandmother to help stretch a strained food budget:

- Substitute one teaspoon of cornstarch if you are short an egg when baking a cake.
- Wrap cheese tightly with a sugar cube in order to prevent mold.
- Rub a half potato on a frying pan if you run out of grease.
- Store your brown sugar in a jar with a piece of bread or apple in order to prevent it from hardening.
- Use a bay leaf in pasta, flour, rice, and dry mixes to keep insects away.
- Sprinkle your fruit with lemon juice to prevent fruit from turning brown.
- Place a saltine cracker in the container of granulated sugar in order to keep it from getting lumpy.

One trick that I use to restore the freshness of pretzels, potato chips, or Tostitos is to heat them up in the oven. To start, preheat the oven to 250 degrees. Place the snacks on a cookie tray. Heat the snacks for 10 minutes. Remove the pan from the oven and let the snacks cool for 15 minutes. Place in an airtight container and your snacks are as fresh as when you first opened the bag.

If my bread has reached the date on the package, I freeze it in a Ziploc bag and then use it for my homemade stuffing/dressing with chicken.

References

General Mills, Inc. 1969. Betty Crocker's cookbook. *Favorite coffee cake*. New York: Golden Press. 55.

General Mills, Inc. 1969. Betty Crocker's cookbook. *Lasagna*. New York: Golden Press. 312.

Perkins, W. L. 1965. The Fannie Farmer cookbook. *Muffins*. Boston: Little, Brown & Company. 313.

Perkins, W. L. 1965. The Fannie Farmer cookbook. *Pizza*. Boston: Little, Brown, & Company. 336.

Chapter 3

Everyday Living

Many of our everyday routines and purchasing practices could be adjusted to make for lots of savings during the year. I have assembled a list of shopping places that I have frequented for the purpose of purchasing clothing and household items over the years.

In addition, I have provided you with a variety of activities around the house in which you can make smart buys and save money every day.

Where to Shop for Bargains on Clothing

When I was growing up, my mother sewed all of her clothes, mine and my two sisters. The fabrics that she bought and sewed were of the highest quality but always on sale. She would shop at the local department stores where she would spend several hours looking at fabrics both for price and quality. By doing this, she was saving money both by the fact that she was making it herself and the sale price of the fabric.

I continued to make my own clothes as well as my three sons' clothes until I was thirty-five years old. Once, I made a fur-lined corduroy coat for my son, which cost a total of $3. As the years passed, money was not as tight, so I began to shop at department stores for my clothes for the first time. Because I was always searching for ways to "save a dime," I looked for items on sale or on clearance. The Hecht Company, an old department store, always had "red dot sales" on the weekends. Sales after Thanksgiving, after Christmas, and again at the end of January into February were also a great time to shop for bargains. Summer sales usually start right after July 4.

Having three sons, I always shopped after the fall and spring seasons for next year's clothes. I would purchase the next size up for the following year.

Now, I find that even the red dot sales at larger department stores are not as good as the everyday shopping in discount stores such as TJ Maxx, Marshalls, and Ross department stores. Several times in the last five years, I have purchased clothing items that I thought were pretty good bargains at a department store only to find the same item in one of these discount stores for ten to twenty dollars cheaper.

Recently, I was shopping at Ross for athletic clothing since I had recently joined a gym. I found items that still had the original manufacturing tags. These prices reflected a much-higher amount than what the Ross tag reflected. In particular, I bought a brand-name pair of three-quarter-length athletic pants with a retail tag of $110.00 and the Ross tag was $9.99.

Some people say they don't like to shop in these discount stores because they cannot find anything. I find that you have to take the time to hunt, and you have to frequent the store often. At times, you will find a really good bargain, and at other times, you may walk out with nothing.

Shoes are another item that can be bought at considerably lower prices at a discount department store or outlet if you take the time to look. Those of us that like shopping in these stores enjoy the hunt, and when we make a find, we feel very good about our efforts and our purchases.

Some of my favorite places to shop are

- TJ Maxx
- Marshalls
- Ross
- Home Goods
- Tuesday Mornings

What Can You Buy at Thrift Stores and Secondhand Shops?

Some people miss the opportunity of a good bargain simply because they are too proud to shop in secondhand stores. Personally, I have the money to shop at expensive department stores, but I won't. I feel this kind of shopping is such a waste of money. I have worked hard for my money, and I want to get the most out of every dollar.

For the past ten years, I have frequented a secondhand store located in Pawley's Island in Myrtle Beach known as Take 2 Resale. I have bought books and videotapes, furniture, clothing, pictures, dishes, and many other items over the past ten years at outstanding bargains when compared to department store prices. You can find these kinds of shops in your local area. I am using these shops as an example of what you can find.

<u>Thrift Stores</u>

I have particularly enjoyed and frequented a thrift shop known as Take 2 Resale at Pawley's Island in Myrtle Beach, South Carolina. Here are a few of the purchases that

I have made over the past ten years and a comparison of what it would have cost me if I had bought the item new.

Thrift Store Item	Retail Price	My Price
Evan Picone Street Length Wool Dress Coat	$400	$65
Forecaster Wool Short Coat	$200	$30
Vera Bradley Matching Jacket and Handbag	$200+	$30
Thomasville Solid Oak Armoire	$1200+	$400
Metal Baker's Rack	$800+	$150
Resin Outdoor Sofa + Cushions	$1200	$300
Resin and Glass Top Coffee Table	$300	$125
Kasper Suit	$250	$25
Hardy Boy Series of Books (25 copies)	$150	$25
Framed, Matted Pictures	$150	$25
Talbot's Sweater (practically new)	$50	$8

Thrift stores abound in all communities. You will need to research your area to find where you can go to shop for "gently" used items such as the ones I have purchased in Myrtle Beach.

Farmers' Markets

Farmers' markets can hold many surprises and treasures just for the price of your time and patience. Again, markets may have many items that have been gently used. These items will cost you a fraction of the cost of what you will pay at department stores. I have bought brand-new pieces of Tupperware that I know would retail for $20 or more and have paid just a dollar. Two items in particular that I have bought are a ring (Jell-O mold) and a container made for basting meat. Over the years, my husband and I have bought many antiques at the farmers' market in Mechanicsville, Maryland. We have spent many hours just perusing in the many different shops and have found many items of interest. I particularly like to pick one thing such as teacups to look for. When shopping, I will purchase only that item. This practice helps to eliminate a lot of impulsive buying but still provides the enjoyment of a good hunt. Over the years, I have collected Bears, Liberty Blue dishes, and a variety of teacups and teapots.

Goodwill Stores

Almost anything that you can think of can be bought at a secondhand store or thrift shop. Some national thrift stores such as Goodwill have excellent bargains and are set up just like a department store. Recently, I was vacationing at Myrtle Beach, South Carolina, and a new Goodwill store had been built on Highway 17 Bypass near Surfside. My husband and I stopped to check out what they might have available. I was amazed at the quality items of clothing that they had displayed. Items were cleaned and displayed on hangers. In addition, the store's organization was set up for easy access and easy-to-find clothing types and sizes. Sections were organized for men, women, and children. The presentation of this store was excellent, and you would not guess that it was a thrift store unless you had read the sign before you entered. In particular, I was amazed at the wonderful selection of babies' and children's clothes that were available. Many labels were brand names. Remember that children from birth to age two barely wear their clothing before they have outgrown them. Great bargains can be had at these types of stores.

I was especially surprised by the number and brand names of blue jeans that they had hanging on racks and their good condition. If your budget is limited, there is no reason to go out and purchase high-priced jeans when you can go to a local Goodwill store.

Yard Sales

My brother Mike and his wife, Jenny, frequent yard sales every Saturday morning. She possesses an eye for decorating, and I have been amazed at some of her finds. Most of what they buy cost between $1 and $10. I have seen them purchase many items that would have been hundreds of dollars in a department store, and they have paid next to nothing for them. Once she purchased a purse for a dollar; and months later, when she went to use it, a fifty-dollar bill was tucked away in one of the zippered compartments.

My brother John and his wife, Connie, faithfully frequented yard sales, hunting for antiques. Again, their finds were amazing. They ran a regular business where they advertised these items on eBay and made a pretty good living.

Selling unwanted household items is another way to get rid of clutter and put a few dollars back in your pocket. Yard sales can be done by yourself or with a neighbor or the neighborhood. Churches and schools also hold yard sales where individuals can purchase a table for $10 to $15. By participating in yard sales, you can take advantage of this activity in helping you to downsize, and you are also engaging in the practice of recycling.

Auctions

Research your local area to find auction houses. Once you start attending regularly, you will begin to see great bargains and values. Before actually buying, take the time to observe the process a few times just to get the feel of how things operate. At the entrance, you will sign up for a number as you enter the auction house. When you make a bid during the auction, your number will be placed on all the items that you purchase throughout the auction process. Whenever you decide that you want to leave, you make your payment with the front desk or office. With larger items, most auction houses will keep them for several days so that you can make arrangements to pick them up later.

Before the auction begins, you should spend about an hour perusing the room to examine the pieces that will be up for auction. Make a list of the items in which you are interested and record the amount you are willing to pay. If you are lucky, your item may not be heavily sought after. If that is the case, you will probably be able to purchase it fairly cheap. The auctioneer begins the bid at a high price, and if there are no bids, he will continue to come down on the price. Your job is to wait to see the lowest price he will accept. At that point, you will begin to raise your card. You may have one or several people bidding against you. The trick is not to spend more than you have allowed yourself. Otherwise, instead of saving lots of money when you are finished, you will have spent too much money. In this buying activity, you will have to exercise self-discipline and self-control. Think about your needs and wants. Remember that over a period of time, some of these items will resurface again, and you will have an opportunity to bid again and obtain your item at a very reasonable price.

Some items that I have seen sold at auctions are

- Longaberger baskets
- Dishes
- Silver
- Tables
- Dressers
- Pictures
- Mirrors
- Bedroom sets
- Baby furniture
- Bicycles/Tricycles
- Outdoor furniture
- Outdoor garden items

The following list contains some of the bargains that I have found at an auction.

Auction Item	Retail Price	My Price
green antique glass stemware (8)	$80	$8
bleached oak coffee table and 2 end tables	$300+	$25
oak dresser	$300	$165
professionally framed pictures	$200+	$5
mirror (4 ft by 4ft)	$200+	$3

Auction Item	Retail Price	My Price
boxes of miscellaneous items	$100	$2.50
dresser	$300	$25
antique oak foyer coat rack	$250	$65
end tables	$125	$10-$25
solid wood rockers	$250	$50
lamps	$100	$25
grill made by George Forman	$40	$2.50

At some of the auctions that I have attended, I have watched the following items sell for fabulous prices.

Auction Item	Retail Price	Going Price
bedroom set (bed, dresser, chest of drawers)	$400+	$25
Oak round table (3 ft diameter)	$300	$40
sofa	$400	$25

Furnishing a Condominium

I recently furnished a two-bedroom condo for under $1,000 buying items at an auction, Goodwill, discount furniture stores, and thrift stores. My husband upholsters furniture as a side business and the upholstered items were recovered with fabric bought at a discount fabric store. One chair, after being reupholstered, cost just $35. The six dining room bamboo chairs cost $15 altogether to recover. One of the lamps was rewired for just $5. Oftentimes, it is just a matter of creativity to come up with very inexpensive ways to decorate your home.

Items purchased at an auction, the goodwill store, or flea market and then used to furnish a condominium.

Auction Item	Retail Price	My Price
4 ft by 4 framed mirror	$200+	$2.50
3 framed/matted gallery pictures	$200+ each	$5.00 each
2 boxes of kitchen bake ware/glasses/silverware	$100+ each	$2.50 each
2 bedroom mirrors (over dressers)	$200+	$10
2 bedroom mirrors	$200	$10
Goodwill Item	**Retail Price**	**My Price**
caned dining room set (glass table top)	$400	$140
living room chair	$300	$10
caned chair	$100	$10

Flea Market/Antique Furniture Item	Retail Price	My Price
2 end tables	$300	$40
1 dresser	$250	$25
2 lamps	$250	$50

Consignment Shops

Many areas have stores that provide the service of selling slightly or gently used clothing or furniture with a small percentage of the sale going to the owner of the shop. This is a good way for you to recoup some of the money you have invested in the item in which you have no further use.

Homemade Greeting Cards

As you all know, the price of a greeting card has gone out of sight over the past five years with most cards costing between three and five dollars. With the tax and the price of the stamp, you can add an additional sixty to eighty cents depending on the size of the card.

When I was growing up, my mother and father always made over the cards and gifts that we had taken our time to make them. A homemade card means a lot to a family member, a grandmother or grandfather when compared to a card that is purchased off the rack. I remember many birthdays, Father's and Mother's Days, and Christmases where we made cards for our parents and our siblings. Most people truly appreciate the message from the heart and the personalization of your gifts and cards.

Dollar Store Greeting Cards and How-to Store the Cards

An average greeting card from a department store can cost anywhere from $3 to $5. I buy most of my greeting cards from many different dollar stores. Cards are usually sold two for one dollar. Your dollar can be stretched a long way by using this practice. I have established a format for storing all-occasion cards that has worked well for me over the past fifteen years. I use a plastic file box that holds 8½" by 11½" file folders. I then label the folders with the identified classification. I will then put the cards in the labeled folders. The folders are then stored alphabetically by the card type. For every three-dollar card that I buy at a department store, I can save two dollars and fifty cents ($2.50). For preprinted labels, see appendix E.

Supermarket Secrets

The healthiest foods can be found on the perimeter in the supermarket. Supermarkets contain many items that are unhealthy, unnecessary for living, or items that are very convenient. If we are faced with tight times, the best way to shop is to stick to the items that are displayed on the outside perimeter of the store. The food items found in this area of the store are meats, vegetables, fruits, and dairy products.

Shopping Lists

Keeping a shopping list is essential in helping you to remember what you need in your household. As you go into a store, this list will assist you in buying only what you "need" and not what you "want." A good idea would be to keep a magnetic tablet on your refrigerator. Each time you run out of something, add it to your list.

Buy in Bulk

The trick to buying in bulk is to use plastic airtight containers to store your foods so that they keep that utmost freshness. Whether you are a two-person household or a many-person household, by storing items properly, anyone can buy in bulk and again save many dollars over the period of a year.

- Bagels
- Bread
- Pretzels
- Chips
- Cookies/Graham Crackers
- Crackers
- Lettuce (Romaine)
- Fruit
- Potatoes

- Frozen Chicken Breast/Thighs/Wings
- Fresh whole chicken
- Fresh hamburger
- Frozen tilapia

What Did It Cost You by the End of the Year?

Many times, we purchase items throughout the week and month at the grocery and convenience stores and don't think much about it because we want it. Take several items that you *buy for convenience* or because you want it right then and *calculate how much it would cost you by the end of the year*. I have made a table to show you how much money certain "nonessential items" would cost you if they were purchased every day for a year. Think about how you could use that money for other expenses such as a down payment for a house or a vacation, or saving for future college expenses for your children etc., if you were to use your self-discipline and do without the "want."

Practice	Daily Cost	Monthly Cost (20 days)	Monthly Savings	Yearly Savings
packing lunch	**$1.25**	**$25**		
lunch out*	$5	$100	$75	$900
bottled water (home)	**$0.20**	**$4.00**	**$16**	**$192**
bottled water (convenience store)*	$1	$20		
1 gallon of water (water bottle, $.75/gal)	**$0.075**	**$1.50**	**$18.50**	**$222**
soda (home, 12 oz)	**$0.25**	**$5.00**	**$20**	**$240**
soda (convenience store)*	$1	$25		
coffee (12 oz, home, $5.00/1 lb)	**$0.20**	**$4.00**	**$21**	**$252**
coffee (12 oz, store*)	$1.25	$25		
Total for the Year				**$1,806**

* Items purchased at convenience or fast-food establishments.

Restaurants

Everyone likes to have a night off from cooking. When going out to eat, there are several ways in which you can save money and still feel like you have had a night off from cooking or the treat of an unexpected breakfast or lunch away from home.

- Save those *coupons* and keep them in a plastic clear sleeve in the door of your car so that they will always be available. Restaurants are constantly running promotions in the newspaper, the Internet, or through flyers in your mail. Recently, I received two coupons in the mail from McDonald's. The promotion was for their new country chicken biscuit sandwich. The customer was required to purchase a medium or large drink with the order. So for approximately $1.25, you could get a sandwich and a drink. Not a bad deal!
- Your beverage order can add a significant amount of extra money to your tab at the end of the meal. Many drinks are running between $2.00 and $3.00. For a family of four at $2.50, that adds up to an extra $10.00. If you add the tax of $1.00 and a tip of $2.00, you have now paid $13.00 dollars for beverages that would cost you about a $1.00 if you had bought them at a local supermarket. Instead, order water when you go out to eat. If you need flavoring, ask for lemon, squeeze it into your water, add sugar, mix it, and you now have *lemonade* that cost you nothing.
- *Alcoholic beverages* typically cost between $3 and $5. When you add the tax and tip to this item, you are paying an additional dollar or two. If you feel you need to have a beer or drink, buy these at the supermarket or liquor store and get a six-pack for the same price that you have spent on one drink or beer at the restaurant.
- *Sharing meals* can be a significant way to cut your bill while at the same time saving you calories. Typically, restaurants provide enough food to feed two or even three people. Order one meal and ask your server to bring an additional plate. You will cut the cost of your meal in half, and you will also have the added benefit of saving additional calories and fat intake.
- Most communities have restaurants that offer *early-bird specials*.

Restaurant Coupons

Chick-fil-A publishes a calendar each year for a cost of approximately $5. Each month, coupons are printed at the bottom of the calendar page to be used during that month for either discounts or a buy one item and get another item free. Restaurant coupons can be additionally found in the newspaper, the Internet, and the mail.

Children's Meals

For the past ten years, I have been using a practice that not only saves me money but also limits my calorie intake by the end of the day. On the occasions when I stop by a fast-food restaurant, I always order from the children's menu. You can significantly lower your fat and caloric intake and save money at the same time. Here are a few examples of the differences in the cost between an adult meal and a children's meal.

Comparison Pricing
Between Child and Adult Meals
At Fast-food Restaurants
(August 30, 2008)

Fast-food Restaurant	Adult Meal	Cost	Child's Meal	Cost	Cost Difference
Checkers	¼ Champ n' Cheese	$5.49	Cheeseburger	$3.69	$1.80
Chick-fil-A	Chicken Sandwich Combo	$5.25	Chicken Nuggets	$2.79	$2.46
	Chicken Strips	$5.59	Chicken Strips	$2.55	$3.04
McDonald's (4-26-09)	Big Mac Combo	$4.91	Cheeseburger	$3.19	$1.72
Wendy's	Hamburger Combo	$4.89	Hamburger	$2.89	$2.00

Try your own cost comparison by visiting a variety of fast-food establishments.

Fast-food Restaurant	Adult Meal	Cost	Child's Meal	Cost	Cost Difference

Cost-Saving Practices (Dos and Don'ts)

Do	Don't
• Buy toiletries in larger sizes. • Buy beverages (coffee, tea, water, soft drinks, etc.) in bulk and carry your own in a cooler or a thermos in your car. • Buy drinking water by the gallon and carry it in your own water bottle as opposed to buying individual bottles of water. • Prepare your meals at home and reserve eating out only for special occasions. • Prepare sandwiches, etc., for long trips to avoid stopping at fast-food restaurants. • Use all leftovers in some manner whether in a soup or stew or smorgasbord night with two or three different choices for family members to choose from.	• Buy small sizes of toiletries. • Buy beverages (coffee, tea, water, soft drinks, etc.) at convenience or fast-food stores. • Eat out if you can avoid it. • Eat at fast-food establishments. • Throw leftovers away. Freeze them if you cannot eat them in a safe, timely manner.

Do	Don't
• Bring water on short road trips.	• Stop to buy bottled water on short errands from home.
• Keep a stash of snacks in a cooler in the trunk of your car for short trips when you get hungry and are not at home to prepare food you have purchased from the grocery store.	• Buy from convenience stores when you are away from home and want a snack.
• Use cloth napkins.	• Use paper napkins.

Cleaning and Conserving without Paper Products

Many people feel they need to buy special furniture polish to clean their furniture. My husband has refinished furniture for years and has denounced the use of polish on furniture. The chemicals contained in these products are not good for your wood furniture. The oils and waxes have a tendency to build up and actually ruin the finish on good wood furniture.

I use old T-shirts, socks and towels as dust cloths. I simply sprinkle a few drops of water on the cloth from the faucet and then do my dusting.

When I use T-shirts for a dust cloth, I cut them in half from the neckline on down, which gives me two pieces. I cut socks halfway down to the heel, and I split an old towel into four sections.

I keep a single plastic trash can in my laundry room and deposit all soiled dust cloths into this container. Once or twice a month, I run these cloths through the washing machine and reuse these same cloths over and over.

I also use these cleaning cloths to clean my hardwood floors. Old towels work well especially to clean hardwood floors. When reusing these cloths, you are practicing the tenets of going green.

Type of Cleaning Cloth	How to Cut
undershirts	Cut in half from the neckline down to the bottom of the shirt.
socks	Cut halfway down from the top of the sock to the heel.
dish towels	Cut in half.
bath towels	Cut in fourths or sixths.
old washcloths	

Recently, I learned that if you mix one part white vinegar and another part water, you can eliminate commercial window cleaners. In addition, you can recycle newspapers and use them in place of paper towels to clean the windows.

Sharing Videos/DVDs

Videos and DVDs are very expensive to purchase at the store. Get together with a family member or a good friend and share your supply of movies. You can also go together to the video store to purchase these items so that you do not duplicate the purchase of the same item. In addition, keep a running list of the movies that you have bought so that you do not purchase the same video twice.

Bartering

Think of a skill that you possess that someone else might be able to use. If you need painting done and someone else needs computer work, you could trade these services without any money passing between you. Bartering was an everyday occurrence in the 1700s and 1800s in our country. During these economically tight times, bartering and trading skills can be an excellent way to help your friends, neighbors, and yourself get through these tough times. Some skills that may be bartered or traded are the following:

- painting
- plumbing
- sewing
- construction (such as building a deck)
- upholstery
- computer-networking problems
- dry-wall work
- electrical work
- hanging cabinets
- hanging new doors or windows
- snow removal
- lawn service
- tax service
- automotive work
- typing
- cooking/baking
- hairdressing and haircuts

Selling on eBay and Downsizing

Selling on eBay is one activity in which I have not engaged personally mostly because I have not taken the time to learn how to do it. I have a sister-in-law and friends who have used this service and have made lots of money over the years. You can get rid of items that are in excellent condition and that you no longer need. This practice can put a little more money back in your pocket. In addition, over the last several years, I have learned the advantages of becoming a minimalist and getting rid of lots of extra "junk" that we have around our homes. I understand this need to be a collector because I have personally engaged in this practice of collecting things from Longaberger baskets to Boyd's Bears to Byers' Choice Dolls. For many years, I could not afford to buy these collectibles. So when I had a little extra money after the kids were finished college, I rewarded myself with many shopping trips with my best friend to buy these things. As I have grown older now, I am tired of them and now want to get rid of them. Having an uncluttered home actually makes you feel more relaxed at the end of a hectic day.

Advertising in Penny Savers and Local Web Sites

In past years, I have advertised a pool table, a woodstove, and real estate with these practices. I sold a regulation pool table for $200 less than when I had purchased it twenty years earlier. My sons and their friends had used it all those years, and the first owner had bought it for his grandchildren who used it for ten years before he sold it to me. This example is another way to engage in the practice of recycling, reusing, and preserving the environment. In addition, I sold a woodstove for just $100 less than what I paid for it after using it for twenty years.

Planting a Garden

When I was first married in the early 1970s, I planted a garden each summer. This activity can help to offset your grocery bill tremendously for about four months of the year. Vegetables that are easy to grow include the following:

- tomatoes
- green beans
- cucumbers
- squash
- lettuce
- zucchini
- cantaloupe

Tomatoes can be used in many economical dishes such as spaghetti, chili, soups, lasagna, etc. Cucumbers can be canned as bread and butter pickles and also used in salads. Green beans can either be canned or frozen to supplement your food bill throughout the winter.

Zucchini can be fried or baked. Squash can be steamed or made into a casserole.

Another advantage of planting a garden is that your family can be treated to fresh vegetables for three to four months of the year where you can be assured that these food items are free of pesticides, which are known to cause cancer.

Planting a garden can also be a great activity in which families can work together and enjoy each other's company.

Planting Fruit Trees

I have planted apple, peach, cherry, and pear trees over the years. An old apple tree grows in my front yard and produces approximately 2-4 bushels of apples in the fall. You can make applesauce, fried apples, apple pizza, apple pie, apple cake, and apple pancakes with apples. See recipes for these dishes in chapter 2. Again, preparing and freezing some of these items can help to lower your food bill over the winter. Remember that a penny saved is a penny earned.

Growing and harvesting your own fruit will insure that your family is having naturally grown food without pesticides and preservatives for a part of the year.

Cheap Entertainment

When times are tight, the first thing you can eliminate from your budget is entertainment outside of the home. Here are some practices that can help to take the bite out of your wallet.

- Using the public library for computer use, borrowing books, videos, and DVDs
- Netflix
- Going to matinees to view new movie releases
- Playing board and card games at home
- Picking up a hobby that is inexpensive such as sewing, needle work, making paper airplanes, and working with your child on the computer either at the library or at home
- Going to the public park
- Enjoying a picnic in your living room with your family

Recently, I was listening to a radio talk show in Washington DC, and a discussion ensued in regard to spending money on expensive toys for our children. Their recommendation per child psychologists is to avoid buying things and spend more time with your family by creating experiences. Going to the park or taking vacations where you spend time with one another are all long-term investments in your family relationships.

Sewing

Another great skill to learn is how to use a sewing machine. At one time, I sewed all my clothes and my sons' clothes when they were little. Now, I enjoy making baby blankets for baby showers and quilts for wedding presents for family and friends. At minimum, everyone should learn how to sew on a button or mend a slight tear in clothing.

Web Sites to Check Out

http://www.sistersofsavings.com
http://www.discountmag.com
http://www.whitefence.com

Chapter 4

Surviving the Energy Crisis and Going Green

The use of oil products in our country is another area that has helped push our country into the economic turmoil that currently exists. Until we find a way to become independent from the need to buy these products from foreign countries, we will continue to run the risk of being held hostage to high fuel prices both for our cars and our homes.

In addition, preserving our environment goes hand in hand with energy conservation. We must consider how we will leave our world to our children, grandchildren, and many generations to come. We are at a turning point, and we must take heed at what scientists and environmentalists are telling us.

Introduction

In the 1940s and '50s, most people owned one car. The father usually worked and used the only vehicle that they owned for transportation each day. Many moms stayed at home and waited to do errands on weeknights or the weekend after the father returned from work. Out of necessity, neighbors called upon each other if they ran out of sugar, flour, or milk (staples). I remember borrowing a cup of sugar or flour or an egg when my mother ran out of these items. After the next trip to the market, my mother would return the borrowed item to her neighbor. You can only imagine how much gasoline this practice saved families in the past. Neighbors helped each other. Maybe now, during this period of tight times, neighbors can once again become closer if they rely on each other more.

Carpools

Years ago, families relied on each other by using the very popular carpools to take kids to Cub Scouts, after-school activities, parks, recreation sports, and many other activities that children participate in outside of school hours. By organizing a carpool with a neighbor who lives close to you, you can save two very precious resources—gasoline and time.

Gasoline

As the months have passed, we have watched the price of fuel climb higher and higher. Several measures have been cited by fuel experts to help lower the cost of each gallon of gasoline that you are using to run your vehicle.

- If you use your cruise control, you can save a percentage of your total cost of a gallon of gasoline at the fuel pump.
- By keeping to the *posted speed limits especially less than 55 mph*, you can also lower the percentage of gasoline that you will need to fill up your tank.
- If you keep your *tires inflated and properly aligned*, this measure can also reduce the amount of fuel that your car will consume.
- *Preventative maintenance* can go a long way in conserving fuel. Oil changes help your motor to run more efficiently and will, in the long run, cost you less for repairs as your vehicle gets older. So tune up your car.
- Purchase the octane that is specified by your car's manufacturer.
- Because cooler gasoline is more compact, fill up your tank in the morning. You'll get more drops of the precious fluid for your dollars.
- The amount of weight carried in your car also affects your gas mileage. Avoid extra cargo in your trunk or car that you are not using such as tool kits, luggage, ski, or bike racks. Store them in your garage until you need them.
- *Using your overdrive* during highway driving additionally reduces fuel consumption.
- Avoid extreme acceleration when getting out on the highway.
- Tailgating promotes unnecessary braking and acceleration.
- Avoid starting your car early before everything is packed in the trunk, the kids are strapped in, and you're ready to go.
- Parking in the shade will reduce the amount of air-conditioning that you use to get your car cool in the summer.
- Using your air-conditioning may increase the amount of gasoline that you use. If possible, try opening your windows especially in city driving when the speeds are slower. You may want to check your owner's manual for specific information about your own vehicle's fuel efficiency when operating the air-conditioning.
- Think about your trips to the grocery or department stores. If you can do without something, wait until your next trip.
- Do your errands on the way to work or on the way home. In this way, your one trip is counting for two purposes. When taking a trip that includes multiple stops, plan your trip in one circle so that you are not driving back and forth to complete your errands.
- Shop with a friend or neighbor to save gasoline.

If all these small measures fail, consider downsizing your vehicle. If you have an SUV or other vehicle with a large engine, you might think about trading your vehicle in for a hybrid or other fuel economy-rated vehicle.

Electricity

Buy energy-saving appliances when you have the opportunity or need to replace an existing appliance. Some older models of refrigerators cost $25 to $30 dollars a month to run. If you own two or three of these appliances, your bill could run between 75 to 85 dollars a month more. The following measures can be taken in your home to reduce your monthly electric bill:

- Try using just one TV at nighttime. It will save money, and you have the added bonus of bringing your family together. In addition, family members learn to share in the selection of the programs to be viewed each evening.
- Turn off the lights when you are not in a room.
- Wash clothes in the late evening since the peak use of fuel is the most during the day. Check with your utility company to find out more about the best times of the day to run your dishwasher and washing machine.
- Unplug computers, TVs, electronics, microwaves, or clocks when not in use. Whenever you see a red light displayed, your appliance or electronic device is still using energy even though it is turned off.

Heating and Cooling

Electric Heat or Air-Conditioning

If you have electric utilities, keeping your thermostat at seventy-five degrees in the summer and sixty-seven degrees in the winter can drastically reduce your monthly utility bill.

By keeping your blinds or drapes closed during the daylight part of the day in the summer, you can additionally save money for air-conditioning by the end of the month.

During the winter, by keeping your blinds or drapes open during the daytime hours especially on sunny days, you can reduce the amount of electricity or fuel oil that you use to heat your house.

I have found that placing a floor fan over the floor vent can actually help to pull the cool air more efficiently from the ducts and then distribute and circulate your air-conditioning better. My family room has an eleven-foot ceiling, and the room is kept much cooler with the floor fan running. Floor fans utilize much less electricity and therefore will reduce your monthly electric bill during the summer.

Woodstoves

In the late 1970s, the country went through a crisis with energy just as we are experiencing now. At that time, my husband and I had a chimney put in our house, and we purchased a Morso Danish woodstove. This stove, placed in our basement, heated almost our entire house. We would start the fire in the woodstove when we got home from work around four or five o'clock in the evening and we would continue to burn it until around 11:00 p.m. This heat would continue through the night, and then the oil-burning furnace would kick in sometime in the morning. We live in a rural area on a wooded lot, and we were able to offset the cost of purchasing wood because of the many trees that were on our property. In addition, we purchased slab wood from the Amish in order to start the fire. Wood needs to be cured and stacked for a period of time before it is used in your woodstove. For this reason, it is important to have logs cut and split six months prior to winter so that it can breathe and dry out. Drying and curing your wood will prevent chimney fires that happen due to a creosote buildup in the chimney flue.

During the ice storm of 1994 in Maryland, we lost electric power for five days. Because of our woodstove, we were able to have heat during these five days. In addition, we took large kettles of snow and ice and melted the snow in the pan on top of the woodstove to use for baths. Having a woodstove is an excellent source of heat in the event of a weather emergency.

To obtain more information on a variety of woodstoves, you can contact the following business Web site *http://www.jotul.us*. In addition, many other companies manufacture woodstoves.

Pellet Stoves

My brother-in-law has used a pellet stove for the past fifteen years to heat his home. His average savings on fuel is $500 a year.

The pellet stove is made of cast iron. Pellet stoves use a biomass product that is made of renewable substances, which are generally recycled wood waste. By using biomass fuel, you may reduce the cost of heating your home through the winter months. It is a form of energy that is good for the environment since it recycles wood waste products for a renewable energy source.

The pellet stove works by putting pellets in a hopper either at the top or the bottom of the stove. Your stove can burn one to two days depending on the size of the hopper in the stove.

Web sites to research further products and dealers for pellet stoves are the following:

http://www.lopfire.com
http://www.Home-Remodeling-Center.com
http://www.hometips.com

Wind Power

Wind farms are becoming popular as a way to harness electricity to run your appliances and to provide heat and air-conditioning to your home. In addition, you can sell back the energy to the power companies when you have used all the energy you need to fulfill your personal use. Using the Web site http://www.tboonepickens.com, you will find many other sites with information on how to build your own small windmill on top of your house as well as information on what the requirements are for building a wind tower on your property. Minimally, you need enough space that if the tower fell, it would not touch any structures or trees in the surrounding areas.

Solar Power

Solar power has been a technology that has been explored and experimented with for many years. New companies are now producing solar panels that can be put on top of your roof to harness energy. Most of these new forms of energy are eligible for energy credits on your income tax return at the end of the year. Check for local, state, and federal guidelines on how to access these energy credits.

Propane Gas

Propane gas is manufactured from petroleum. It is used for cooking inside and for outdoor grills and smokers. In addition, it is used to provide energy for propane fireplaces in your home.

To obtain more information on custom fireplaces for a variety of fuels, contact the following business Web sites or telephone numbers:

http://www.travisbuilder.com or call 1-800-654-1177
http://www.lennox.com or call 1-800-9-LENNOX

Cost Comparisons for Alternative Fuel Products

Fuel	Measured by	Appliance Efficiency	Cost per Million BTU	Cost Per Year
wood pellets	$259 /ton	80%	$19.74	$1,381.80
hardwood	$180 /cord	60%	$15.00	$1,050.00
fuel oil	$4.50 /gal	78%	$41.81	$2,926.70
electricity	$0.13 kwh	100%	$38.00	$2,667.00
natural gas	$1.77 / therm	78%	$22.14	$1,549.00
propane gas	$4.20 /gal	78%	$58.96	$4,127.20

These calculations were based on an average BTU load of 70M per year.

The calculations were provided by http://www.pelletheat.org through the Tri County Hearth and Patio Center in Waldorf, Maryland, at http://www.heatbyfire.com.

Some Interesting Facts

Did you know that

- the energy saved from recycling one aluminum can will run your TV for three hours (http://www.freecycle.com);
- replacing old-model air conditioners with Energy Star appliances can reduce the cost of your energy bill by 20 percent (Energy Star);
- transportation uses 67 percent of the oil consumed in the United States (United States Department of Energy);
- America uses nine million barrels of gasoline daily (Alliance to Save Energy); and that
- many appliances and electronics such as microwaves, televisions, cordless phones, Internet, and VCRs use energy when they are turned off?

Working toward a Green Environment

Going Green is a concept in which you look for ways to reuse, recycle, and renew in order to preserve the environment and the one earth on which we all live, work, and play. Many ideas are floating around for all of us to try in order to help us do our part in helping to preserve the one earth that we have. We must look for ways in which to protect our environment so that it is still here for future generations.

Reusable Market Bags

Many markets and local stores are selling reusable bags for a dollar. Not only will you be helping the environment, but you will not have to figure out what to do with all those plastic bags that you bring home from the market and department stores each week.

Consignment Shops

Most communities have consignment shops where you can sell gently used clothing, toys, and household items. The store takes a percentage of the sale, and you get to keep the rest. This measure is a nice way to get rid of things you can no longer use and, at the same time, make a little extra cash.

Throwaway Nation

We live in a society where people think they have to constantly buy or possess new things. Little thought goes into the idea of fixing or mending household items when they break or replacing a button that is missing on a piece of clothing or clothing that needs a few stitches. We purchase food items from the supermarket in plastic containers and throw away the containers after they are empty. These can be reused to store other household items such as hardware, stickpins, safety pins, buttons, paper clips, coins, etc. We need to look for ways that we can reuse many household containers.

Ways to Reuse Plastic Containers

- Store leftovers after dinner.
- Take food for lunch.
- Use large 4-lb pretzel containers to store plastic bags from department stores or supermarkets, dust cloths, or flower seeds for the next year.
- Use plastic 3-lb containers from nuts for the same purpose as above. These containers can also be used to store flower bulbs.
- Use rubbermaid or plastic containers such as cool whip containers to store leftovers in the refrigerator and the freezer.

Christmas Gifts Using Glass Jelly Jars

Save your fancy glass jelly/jam jars throughout the year. At Christmas, you can purchase chocolate-covered almonds or chocolate-covered raisins in bulk (or any other chocolate candy or nuts). These can be put into the jars and tied with a ribbon to make an economical Christmas gift. As my mother always told us as children growing up, that "giving a gift is more about the thought than about how much it cost."

Did You Know You Were Going Green When You

- frequent an auction house and buy already-used items;
- reuse your plastic grocery bags to line small wastebaskets in bedrooms or bathrooms;
- buy at thrift shops;
- have your furniture reupholstered;
- donate to thrift stores;
- carry your lunch in a cooler or thermal bag;
- reuse plastic containers from the grocery store such as cool whip containers, sour cream, cottage cheese containers, etc.;
- reuse glass products such as mayonnaise jars, jelly jars, Harry and David glass containers;
- wash clothes in cold water;
- bike to work; and
- reuse plastic and paper bags?

Laundry

Using bath towels two to three times instead of once can save one or two loads of extra laundry a week. Over the period of one year, this can calculate into fifty to one hundred extra loads of laundry.

Web Sites

http://www.freecycle.com
http://www.dealcatcher.com
http://www.BlackFriday.com
http;//www.BoonePickens.com
http://www.tips@stretcher.com
http://www.TheDollarStretcher.com

Chapter 5

Finances

A penny saved is a penny earned.
—Benjamin Franklin

"A penny saved is a penny earned" is a very old saying (over two hundred years). This saying means that a person who takes the time to discipline himself to save rather than spend everything he has, truly has exhibited self-discipline and has earned that money that has been saved. *Saving is hard work and sacrifice.* Many times, at the end of the day, when I have finished a hard day's work, I would rather go out to dinner than go home and prepare a meal. However, I know that eating out is one of the biggest wastes of money. So I take the little extra time to either fix a quick meal, eat leftovers, or take something out of the freezer that was leftover from another meal that I have prepared previously. In everything that we do, there are costs. When you choose to make one purchase, you use or lose an opportunity to make another purchase. Money is not limitless; there is a bottom to the well, and money doesn't grow on trees as old sayings go. Money will eventually run out if we do not plan and think about how we are spending it.

How Did We Get to This Place Called Economic Crisis?

Now that the stock market has dropped dramatically, many houses are in foreclosure. Families are declaring bankruptcy, and many families are not living in the lifestyles that they have been accustomed due to the tightening of their belts. *What did cause this crisis that we currently seem to be embroiled?*

Financial experts have cited more than just the stock market, the oil, and mortgage companies for the problems our country faces. Some of this blame can be placed on all of us and our many consumer practices that were unrealistic. Here are a few of them:

- Lack of self-discipline with credit cards
- Our need for immediate gratification
- Greedy bankers, loan officers, and financial brokers
- Greedy speculators in land and housing markets
- Greedy home owners
- Buying houses that were beyond our means
- Lack of using the practice of saving money
- Buying on credit rather than saving for big ticket items
- Leasing cars that were beyond our means to buy

Several economic principles (needs, wants and opportunity costs) should be practiced as we go about our daily business of living, paying our bills, and buying big-ticket items that generally are considered luxuries. These principles have been introduced and taught to third graders in the state of Maryland since the early 1990s. I know that this knowledge has been assessed in our state for over ten years through the Maryland School Performance Assessment Program. When these concepts were first introduced, I wondered myself why these principles were being taught so early. Today, after our financial collapse in the United States, I can't help but think if everyone knew these principles of *needs, wants*, and *opportunity costs;* we might not be in the predicament that we currently find ourselves in. I will take a few moments to examine each one of these principles in isolation.

Needs and Wants

The principle of needs and wants is a simple decision-making system to help us determine how to spend our money especially when our budgets are tight. As a result, we will have to give up some things that we think we want but these things are really not necessities. In order to exercise these principles, for myself, I would make a simple table with needs on one side and wants on the other. Then, I might make a list of the things that I would like to have and determine if they are a need or just something that I want.

Use the following table to make a list of all the expenditures that you make for one week. Indicate the date, the item, and how much it cost. At the end of the week, identify whether the purchase was a real need or just a want. Add the needs and the wants to determine how much they total. At this point, you will be able to determine from the want column how much money you have spent unnecessarily throughout the week.

Weekly Log of Expenditures

Date	Item	Cost	Need	Want

Opportunity Cost

Opportunity cost is another concept that we have been teaching our children in the Maryland public schools since the 1990s. This concept is all about what you have to give up when you make a decision to purchase or invest in one item over another. For instance, your family wishes to buy a new television and also wants to go on a family vacation to the beach. The cost of each is $700. Your family cannot afford to do both things. They must decide which is the most desirable at that moment. As a family plans their budget, it is important to take in consideration opportunity cost because no family has an endless pot of gold or a money tree. This concept is important to be aware of as it helps us to make the important decisions about financial matters that can have serious consequences.

Budgets

Now that we have discussed the concept of needs and wants, we can talk about how to begin to develop a budget. Starting with where you really need to spend your money first, you will want to list all your ongoing monthly bills, which may include the following:

Monthly Household Bills/Budget	Amount
mortgage or rent	
homeowner's insurance	
monthly property tax	
car payment	
car insurance	
health insurance (if applicable)	
electric bill	
telephone (landline)*	
cell phone*	
home fuel bill	
average monthly gasoline bill	
water	
sewage	
cable TV/Internet*	
emergencies	minimum $50
savings	minimum $25
miscellaneous	
miscellaneous	
Total	

food   total of your monthly take-home income
         - monthly bills
         money left for food budget	

entertainment* (not a necessity)	

Note: (*) Can be deleted from your budget in an emergency such as unemployment

For the purpose of developing a balanced budget, we will not add any credit card debt after adding all these figures. By doing this budget, you will be able to see how little money you have to charge purchases if you want to pay off your debt at the end of each month.

Balancing a Checkbook

When you get your paycheck every week or two weeks, you should first make certain that you pay yourself (savings and retirement funds) and your household bills before you spend any money on entertainment or going out to eat. Here is where the lesson on needs and wants comes into play. We often spend money on wants and then don't have enough to pay the needs. This practice results in people using credit in order to make all ends meet. In addition, if the person does not save anything, the action manifests itself in poor credit ratings and never being able to have enough money saved to put down as collateral for buying a home.

For those who have never used a checkbook, I have included a sample of a blank check and a check that has been filled out for a purchase.

Blank Check

Blank Check

2114.
Date_____
Payable to:_____Amount_____
_____ Dollars
Note_____   _____
Signature

Completed Check

2114.
Date October 10, 2008
Payable to   John Doe _____Amount $15.00
Fifteen_____ $\frac{00}{100}$ Dollars
Note: Birthday Present, Johnny   Mary Smith
Signature

Financial Planning

Paying off credit card debt is one of the first things you should begin to do if you have not presently planned for your future. Banks and credit card companies are working to eliminate customers who are paying only minimum payments or who are late paying their bills. When you are late for a credit card payment, a huge surcharge can be added and your interest rate could go up to as high as 30 percent permanently. Recently, credit card companies have been sending out new agreement notices to their card members. Cardholders are being told that their current interest rates are essentially going to be raised to the primate rate plus 10.99 percent. This translates into a much higher interest rate of 14 percent or higher for the monthly balance of your credit card debt. The only way you can reject this offer is by calling or writing the company to turn down this new agreement. In addition, by refusing to accept these new terms, your credit card becomes no longer usable. *Beware of these notices.* These notices come in a trifold, and it is very important for you to read all the fine print. Otherwise, you will be stuck with a high interest rate, which will make it more difficult for you to pay off the balance of your debt.

The second phase of financial planning is to contribute regularly to your *personal savings account.* When I was in my twenties, I started by saving $25 a pay period. For approximately fifteen years thereafter, each new annual pay raise that I received, I put in the savings account. Currently, I contribute $800 a pay period ($1,600 a month) into a savings account. This practice has permitted me to always have something to fall back on when emergencies arose. In addition, when my three sons each became of college age, I literally had enough money that I was regularly saving that would then become the monthly payment for college tuition and room and board.

I practiced the same concept with a Christmas fund. I started with $25 a pay period, which gave me $600 at the end of the year. I added $25 to this amount periodically and I now save $250 a month, which nets me over $3,000 in November to spend on Christmas or other big-ticket items that we might want. This practice has saved me from ever using a credit card for Christmas purchases over the past twenty years.

The third phase of financial planning is to begin investing money for *retirement.* This is one area in which I believe I should have started earlier. It is never too early to begin investing for that day when you will no longer work either because you choose not to or because you can't. I was given the advice to begin investing in a 403B when I was thirty-two. I waited until I was forty-eight to begin this kind of investment. The longer you wait, the less time you will have for your money to grow. Although many people are reluctant to invest in the markets with the current economic crisis, there is never a better time to invest in mutual funds or stocks. Stocks are very low in price now. Certainly, you must be cautious at this time, by choosing a reputable financial planner to help you with these financial matters. Many companies offer these services, but it will be important for you to find out which advisors give you advice without getting a portion of your investment. You have to speak up and ask when interviewing for a financial planner. The big thing to remember when investing in the market is when the market declines, you must be willing to wait it out for the recovery. If you are five to ten years away from retirement, you need to begin moving some of your money into less risky or safer investments such as a fixed-income fund. A market decline can take up to ten years to recover and then begin to rise back to its original amount before the decline (Orman 2009).

Electronic Bill Payment

They say that "an old dog cannot be taught new tricks." I turned sixty this past summer, and I have just begun to pay all my bills electronically through my bank in this past year. I have figured that I am saving almost $200 a year on postage. The amount of time it takes to pay all my bills has been significantly reduced. Typically, I would sit down for forty-five to sixty minutes twice a month to perform this dreaded task. Now, it takes me no longer than fifteen minutes every two weeks. I no longer have to address envelopes, put postage and return address labels on the envelope, and then take the bills to the post office for mailing. In addition, as long as you have access to the Internet, you can pay your bills anywhere.

The Saving Money Practice

Establishing a routine practice for saving money from each pay period is extremely important in wise financial planning. In addition, you are modeling for your children the importance of saving for the future. It is alright for your children to hear you *say no* that you cannot afford to make a certain purchase that falls in the "wants" category. In this way, they will understand themselves when they are adults that people must live within their means and within a budget (See the section entitled "Financial Planning" in this chapter for an example).

A Web site to help you with savings is http://www.Smartypig.com.

Savings Plans for Children

The practice of learning to save should start as a child. If you have younger children, begin the basics of teaching them how to save even when they only have access to just a little bit of money. Each time your child receives money either as an allowance or as a gift from family members and friends, encourage him/her to save a portion of that amount. For amounts that are under five dollars, a good rule of thumb would be maybe 10 percent of the total. Give your child a jar or a piggy bank to save their money. Monthly or bimonthly, take a trip to the bank and let your child deposit his money in a savings account. Encourage your child to buy savings bonds as the money begins to accumulate in the savings account. In this activity, your child will enjoy watching his/her money grow.

Savings Plans for Single Adults

As a single person, saving money can be more difficult because there is only one salary to pay for all of the household debt. If it is possible and you have the space in your home, condo, or townhouse, you should consider renting out one of your bedrooms to help offset your monthly cost. This extra money can be put away into your personal savings account, your savings for six months of salary reserve or your retirement accounts.

Savings Plans for Married Couples

Typically, one spouse is better with finances than the other. In my home, it was me. I can remember the first few months when my husband and I were newlyweds. A system was not in place, and I waited for him to take care of the bills, and he waited for me to take care of paying the bills. Consequently, we were late on some payments in those first months simply because one person had not stepped up to the plate. Very quickly, the routine of paying the bills became my job.

Money can be a leading issue that can make or break a marriage. Early in your relationship, even before your marriage, you should spend some time together discussing how the allocation of money and spending was viewed in each of your homes. This basic philosophical view of money can be very different for different families. Remember that each family has its own culture on this topic/issue and many others that face you daily.

In order to really discover how each thinks about money, I have developed a list of ideas that you might discuss. The following topics are up for discussion:

- how you each view the way in which you save and spend money
- identify common individual goals and goals that may be different
- how much money you need to save for your six-month reserve account
- the use of credit cards
- what is a need and what is a want
- saving for retirement (retirement plans, 401K, 403B, etc.)
- how and when to spend money on entertainment such as eating out, going to the movies, partying, and vacations
- long-range goals and purchases such as a home and college savings plans for children

You might even consider going to a financial consultant at your local bank simply to obtain some advice. This service is typically free to customers at the bank.

Taxes and Tax Breaks

If you own a home, it is important to itemize and claim all the deductions that you can at tax time. Historically, I have always claimed zero deductions or even a negative deduction for a regular pay period. I have also elected to have an additional $100 taken out of my bimonthly check. This practice protects me from having to pay the federal government during tax season for underpaid taxes. When I get a tax return, I can use it to purchase something special for that particular year or just invest it in a savings account. Some financial planners will advise against this practice because your money is not growing. However, I like the peace of mind that comes with knowing that I will be getting a tax refund in April of the following year.

Some itemized deductions you can take are

- interest on a home mortgage;
- taxes on a vehicle purchased during that tax year;
- dependents (anyone living in your household);
- charitable contributions (church, Goodwill, American Cancer Society, etc.);
- property taxes;
- mileage to a second job;
- interest on a home equity loan;
- the cost of energy improvements (additional insulation, solar power, energy-efficient appliances, energy-efficient windows, etc., these are based on particular tax years); and
- interest on school loans.

The use of tax programs such as Turbo Tax or Tax Cut can be very beneficial in helping you to complete your taxes. In addition, if you use the same program each year, the program will allow you to bring up what you did from the previous year. This information is then carried over to the current year's tax program.

Buying a Car

For the first ten years that my husband and I were married, we always *purchased used vehicles.* My husband and I were 35 and 32 respectively before we had our first new vehicle. This practice is another way you can save a lot of money over the years. Now that I am approaching retirement years, my husband and I have discussed buying used cars again. When you buy a new vehicle and drive it out of the parking lot, you immediately lose thousands of dollars in value.

Let's take a look at the amount of money you can save when comparing the purchase of a used car versus a new car over a period of forty years until 2050. Suppose you buy a vehicle every seven years.

Year	Used Car	New Car
2010	$12,000	$25,000
2017	$13,000	$26,000
2025	$14,000	$28,000
2032	$14,000	$28,000
2039	$15,000	$29,000
2046	$16,000	$30,000
Total	**$84,000**	**$166,000**
Difference	**$82,000**	

The difference calculates to $82,000 more spent on new cars as opposed to used cars. This amount of money, if invested in a retirement account, could have a significant impact on how you will live in your golden years.

Buying a House

Not too many years ago, banks required that the buyer have collateral for the purchase of a new home. This practice consisted of the buyer having at least 10 to 20 percent of the total value of the home before a loan could be processed. The collateral could be in two forms: either cash in hand or the ownership of the land. The land had to have the equivalent value of 10 to 20 percent of the value of the mortgage that was to be taken on building the house. Today, banks permit you to purchase homes and cars without putting any money down. The problem with this practice is that the banker does not know whether the purchaser has the capability of saving money from paycheck to paycheck for such a big purchase. If the buyer has 10 to 20 percent of the money to back their mortgage, it is obvious to the banker that this buyer has the ability to save and put money away.

Even if a bank does not require a 10 to 20 percent deposit, it is a good practice for buyers to have a substantial amount of money saved prior to making such a big purchase. In addition, if the buyer has been saving a certain amount over a period of a year or two, the buyer also knows that he can make those payments when the mortgage is due each month. This practice of saving money and not spending everything that you make takes self-discipline and is a characteristic that is very important in being money-wise and keeping your own household in order.

I remember when my husband and I were first married and getting ready to make the ultimate purchase of a home in the early 1970s. We were both teachers, and in the first two years of our marriage, we saved enough money to purchase our property, which cost $5,200 back then. Today, that seems like a small amount of money, but our salaries were each just $6,500 a year.

We decided to build a "Ridge" home, which would save us lots of money because we would be doing most of the work ourselves. All the materials were provided by the company to build the home. The company came in and took care of building the basement and the outside walls and roof. Everything else on the inside of the house, which included the electric, plumbing, dry wall, insulation, doors, appliances, and floors, had to be completed by us. When choosing the model of our home, I remember that I wanted a two-story home that cost $24,000. My husband said it was too much since I had elected to stay home with our children for the next several years. The home that we selected was $17,900. Again this seems like such a little bit of difference between the two homes, but it represented a 25-percent difference in what our mortgage would be.

It is important as a young buyer to sit down and take into account all your expenses that you have to put out in a month's time when you buy a home (See section on sample budget in this chapter). After making a budget, you must decide if you have enough money coming in monthly to make all those payments. *It is far better to buy a home that is smaller than to buy a larger one where at the end of the month you have no extra cash in your pocket. You will be house poor!*

Saving for the Future

Financial planners have always given the advice to save enough money for six months of your salary in case you ever lose your job because of illness, a recession or a slow economy. I know that making this commitment to save this amount of money is very hard when your salary seems to be just enough to get by with each month. However, you must find a way to have this cushion or buffer.

Look to see if there are any small changes you can make that, in the long run, will help you to save a few dollars here and there. In the chart below are some simple examples of daily practices that can save you money by the end of the month. Multiply that by twelve and see how much more money you can save by the end of the year.

As you look at the following chart, take particular note of the overall cost of just four items by the end of the year. By changing your practice of depending on convenience as opposed to taking the extra time to plan and to be mindful of your needs during the day, you can save almost $2,000 a year just for one person. Multiply that by two people in the household, and you have now saved $4,000 in a year. Multiply that figure by ten years, and you now have $40,000, which can be a significant down payment for a home or a nest egg for retirement. You are not denying yourself of the cup of coffee, the can of soda, and the bottle of water. You are still having the coffee except you are depending on the fact that you are preparing your coffee yourself and you are bringing it in a thermos. For water, you can buy it in packages of 24-36 or prepare a water bottle using the gallon container of water in your refrigerator. A little extra effort, planning, and time each day can yield significant savings by the end of the year.

Practice	Daily Cost	Monthly Cost (20 days)	Monthly Savings	Yearly Savings
packing lunch	**$1.25**	**$25**		
lunch out*	$5	$100	$75	$900
bottled water (from home)	**$0.20**	**$4**	**$16**	**$192**
bottled water (convenience store)*	$1	$20		
1 gallon of water (water bottle) $.75 gal	**$0.075**	**$1.50**	**$18.50**	**$222**
soda (home) 12 oz	**$0.25**	**$5**	**$20**	**$240**
soda (convenience store)*	$1	$25		
coffee 12 oz at home (1 lb $5.00)	**$0.20**	**$4**	**$21**	**$252**
coffee 12 oz in store*	$1.25	$25		
Total for the Year				**$1,806**

College Plans for Children or Grandchildren

Begin saving for your children or grandchildren from the day they are born. Diversify the way in which you invest your money. Some ways in which you can begin to save are

- buying bonds (they double in twelve years and can be used for education without paying any taxes on the gain);
- buying property or real estate for rentals;
- asking grandparents to give savings bonds for birthdays and Christmas (They will add up quickly over the subsequent eighteen years.);
- investing in cash value life insurance (Not included in federal aid); and
- purchasing Roth IRAs (principal is not taxed or penalized for college).

Savings Bonds for Children

Savings bonds come in increments of $50, $100, $200, $500, and $1,000. You may purchase bonds at your local banking establishment. When you buy a bond, you must have your child's or grandchild's social security number. You will be asked to name a co beneficiary, usually the parent. When you buy a $50 bond, you pay just $25. In the twelve years to maturity, it will increase in value to the amount stated on the bond. The bank will give you a gift card that you can give to the child that acknowledges that she/he will receive the bond in the next six weeks.

Diversifying Your Portfolio/Assets

A key strategy in financial planning is diversifying your portfolio. At this economic time in our country, there is no greater evidence that this strategy can help offset the losses in any one area.

Within your portfolio, the following items may be included:

- Personal savings (car and house insurance, vacations, televisions, etc.)
- Emergency savings (household needs)
- Savings for six to eight months reserve in case of job loss
- Christmas fund
- Retirement accounts such as 403B, 401K, 457 (retirement)
- Money markets, CDs, savings bonds (retirement and college savings)
- Real estate

I have invested in most of the above plans or strategies. I have lost a great deal of money in the stock market through mutual funds in several 403B accounts. However, I know that even during the Depression years from 1930 to 1945, if people had left their money in the stock market, the financial graphs and charts show that in ten years, those stocks actually regained their losses and went on to produce gains for their investors.

Though you hear lots of news about the real estate market and how people have been greedy with the practice of buying and turning over property, this measure is still effective if done cautiously and without spending money in which you do not have. You must still live within your means, but again, it is about saving for your future. I have been very successful in my *investments in the real estate market*. Keep in mind that I am an educator and my husband is a civil servant for the government. Over the years, we have been able to send three sons to college and still save money for the future. Though my salary is much higher today, just fifteen years ago, I made $42,000 as an elementary school principal. On our salaries, we have made the following investments in the real estate market, and these investments have shown the following gains:

Year	Investment	Gain
1997	**Condominium in Myrtle Beach, South Carolina** We had about $17,000 from my husband's inheritance. We knew that over a few years, this money could easily have been flitted away. We bought a condominium for $76,000. Over the years, it has been a tax write-off as well as a great many family vacations, which hold a wealth of wonderful memories.	• Tax write-off for interest and property taxes • Vacation for my parents for the past ten years in the spring and fall • Honeymoons for my sons and several nieces and nephews • Vacations for my sons and their friends
2009	Though the market is terrible now, we have still managed to sell the condo for $105,900. We have lost $50,000 in value compared to the prices just three years ago, but we still broke even after accounting for a fully furnished condo. Hence, the caution to buy real estate but not with the intention of flipping every two years.	
2003 2005	Purchased property (land) in Myrtle Beach for $78,000 Sold property for $185,000 Profit of $107,000, actual profit of $65,000 after capital gains tax and South Carolina state tax for second home	$107,000
2005	Purchased golf-front property in Myrtle Beach for $81,000 and built a house on the property	Value: $375,000 Owe: $20,000

Over the last ten years, we have made extra payments on the condominium whenever we had extra cash, whether it was from tax refunds, from profits on property sales, monetary gifts from family, or extra money from our Christmas fund, etc. When we recently sold our condominium, we owed just $9,000 to the bank. By the time we sold our property in 2005 and the condominium in 2009, we were able to end up with just a $20,000 mortgage on the house we built in Myrtle Beach.

Demystifying the Vocabulary of Financial Planning

Over the years, I have found that the discussion of financial planning can be very intimidating especially when looking at all the potential plans in which one can invest. Even after buying two books on this subject fifteen years ago, I still have a difficult time understanding all this financial jargon. I have put together a list of financial terms with the help of a friend and financial advisor to help simplify some of this vocabulary.

Vocabulary Term	Explanation
401 (k)	Contributions made to a retirement account through your employer's payroll system (Employer is not a nonprofit organization/business). These contributions are taken out of your salary without being taxed. The advantage of this type of retirement savings is that you don't pay taxes until after you withdraw the money when you are over 59 ½, and you are typically receiving a lower income. The lower income makes your tax rate lower. Asset allocation is usually divided into five different categories. These categories represent fixed income, small cap mutual funds, mid cap mutual funds, large cap mutual funds, and international stocks.
Roth 401 (k)	A contribution-based retirement account. Money can be allocated to this account after taxes have been paid. Many companies do not yet offer this account because of the amount of work it takes the employer to maintain these accounts.
403 (b)	Contributions made to a retirement account through your employer's payroll system (Employer is a public school or a nonprofit tax-exempt organization or business). Your contributions are made before your earnings are taxed.
Roth 403 (b)	This account contains specialty, international, and socially responsible stocks. Roth 403 (b) is the same as the 403 (b) except that contributions are made after tax and when received after sixty-five years of age, there is no tax at that time.
457	Contributions made to a retirement account through your employer's payroll system.

Vocabulary Term	Explanation
Annuity	An annuity is a contract sold by an insurance company. An annuity is tax-deferred. Annuity policies are bought to guard against you outliving your other assets for retirement.
Asset Allocation	Represents the way in which you distribute your money between stocks, bonds, and cash/stable value options.
Bonds	Issued by corporations or government agencies. May be purchased at your local bank. A good source of savings for college tuition with a fixed rate of income. (*low risk*)
Cash/Stable Value	Similar to bonds with low returns and are held for a much shorter period of time than bonds.
Certificate of Deposit (CD)	CDs may be purchased at a bank or savings and loans. They are purchased for either short- or long-term investment. CDs offer higher rates of return than many other investments. A penalty exists if a CD is cashed in before its maturity date.
Diversify Portfolio	A variety of investments, which gain and lose at different times. Along with investments involving banks and insurance companies, the real estate market can also be included in a diversified portfolio.
Financial Advisor	A person or organization employed by an individual or mutual fund to manage assets or provide investment advice.
Fixed Income	A certain percentage that usually maintains consistency throughout the life of the investment. Example: Savings Accounts and Bonds
Money Market	An investment which usually shows a lower rate of return when compared to some other investments. They are generally a very safe investment.
Mutual Funds	Mutual funds are usually purchased from an investment company, which raises money from shareholders and invests in a group of assets. The company makes money by selling shares of the fund to the public.
Portfolio	Represents all the ways in which your money is distributed such as real estate, banks, savings, the stock market, mutual funds, etc.
Securities	An investment instrument, which is not an insurance policy or fixed annuity
Real Estate	Houses, condominiums, or land
Stocks	Represent a share in the ownership of a company. Stocks pose a greater risk than a bond or cash/stable value.

Vocabulary Term	Explanation
Small Cap Stock	Represents the smallest 2,000 stocks of the Russell data series, which includes 98 percent of the investable U.S. equity market
Mid Cap Stocks	Represents the 400 stocks intended to the middle capitalization sector of U.S. equity markets
Large Cap Stocks	Represents stocks in large-capitalization companies and includes 500 of the largest stocks in the United States
Treasury Bond	A treasury bond is issued by the United States government and backed by full faith and credit. These bonds are exempt from state and local taxes. Treasury bonds pay interest every six months.

Developed in consultation with Christopher J. King, financial planner, with the company of Raley, Watts, & O'Neill in California, Maryland

References

Orman, Suzi. 2009. *2009 action plan: keeping your money safe and sound.* New York: Spiegel McGray.

Chapter 6

Keeping Healthy and Avoiding Stress

During stressful times, it is important for you to have a plan to reduce your stress. Research has shown that stress is a top factor in shortening a person's life as well as causing many health issues such as high blood pressure, heart attacks, and strokes. Exercise and a healthy diet can help to reduce or alleviate stress. In addition to healthy daily living practices, health insurance is a must for a family. This chapter will explore both healthy living and health insurance alternatives.

When Out of Work

What do you do when you find you are unexpectedly laid off from your job? Even more than the loss of the weekly paycheck comes the loss of the health benefits that are tied to a salary. There are several important measures in regard to health insurance that you must take as soon as possible. You must make some decisions about health insurance so that you and your family are protected during the period when you are no longer employed with a company that provided you and your family health insurance prior to the unemployment period.

Cobra

The first thing that you need to know is that you are entitled for a period of time, usually three to six months, to continue purchasing insurance with the company from which you were being covered. This phenomenon is known as Cobra. The coverage is not free (you must now pay the full premium price); however, having health insurance coverage will give you a little peace of mind for a while. You may need to ask for help from family or use unemployment benefits to help with this expense.

Talk to your insurance company, and you may be able to negotiate a different plan that will cover you during this interim period for a lower price.

If you do not have the money to pay this sometimes-very-expensive premium, you may elect to do several other things during the interim.

Piggyback on Your Spouse's Insurance

In the past, many companies have offered their employees coverage for their dependents at a very small payment. Today, because insurance is so expensive, many companies and corporations offer a reduced rate of insurance to their employee and not to members of their families. If your wife or husband happens to work for a company that will pick you up on their insurance plan for a limited amount of premium, this option is very good. You may have a reduced rate of payment for this option.

High-Deductible, Lower-Premium Insurance Plans

When you lose your health insurance with the company or business you were with, it is important to begin immediately researching insurance plans that can help offset the potentially high cost of medical bills. In particular, you need to be covered for the unseen, catastrophic-type medical emergencies. You can choose plans that have $1,000 to $10,000 deductible, which makes your out-of-pocket charge high but covers you for bills that could lead to thousands of dollars in bills.

When purchasing high-deductible insurance, your monthly premium will be very low in comparison to plans that cover low co-pays to doctor's offices or prescription-drug medicines needed during this period. *Don't sit back and do nothing.* You must make sure that you and your family are protected and covered minimally for catastrophic medical emergencies. Otherwise, you will be paying for the rest of your life on huge medical bills if you experience a situation, which incurs thousands of dollars in medical expenses. The national news has reported recently that many family bankruptcies are directly related to huge medical bills.

Looking for a Job

Begin immediately putting out resumes either online or in person to businesses similar to your own. If you find that your particular business was hard-hit by the recession, you may consider applying for jobs outside your typical comfort level. Even if you have to work two or three jobs, the goal is to bring in as much money as possible so that you can pay your bills.

Retraining

After this recession, there will be some types of businesses that will never come back. These businesses will be obsolete because their function will no longer be in line with protecting the environment or manufacturing products that will be economically feasible for the populace. You might want to research the up-and-coming fields. Visit your local community college to talk to an advisor or counselor about what fields are most in demand. The forecast at this time is that jobs dealing with alternative fuels that are good for the environment and jobs in the health care fields will be the most sought after by employers for the next fifteen years. Consider going back to school so that you will be prepared for the next round of careers that will make you and your skills marketable.

Time on Your Hands

Find things to do around the house, for neighbors or family. It is important to keep your body and mind healthy during this period of transition and stress. You might consider finding odd job from people that you know. Other activities to engage in are

- reading a book;
- taking a walk;
- volunteering at a school, hospital, or church;
- cleaning the house;
- cleaning out a closet or some area of the house that needs it;
- washing the windows;
- creating or making something;
- baking bread or desserts;
- using the Internet to search for jobs;
- raking leaves, cleaning your gardens;
- writing letters to friends or family that you have not been in contact;
- attending job fairs; and
- developing more than one resume with a slant toward different jobs.

The point is that you must keep yourself busy in order to keep your mind from wandering and dwelling on the negative situation in which you find yourself in.

Exercise

Join a gym to use up some of your free time. Even though a gym cost money to join, talk to the owner to see if you can work out some kind of arrangement for a lower fee. In addition, the owner/manager may even make a deal where you can barter a service for the waiver of a fee.

If you cannot join a gym, find exercise videos that work you through an exercise routine.

If your neighborhood terrain permits, walk or ride a bicycle each day.

Diet

What you eat and how much you eat can increase during this period where you are not constructively employed during the week.

- Make sure that you lower the amount of empty calories you take in such as sodas, candy, cookies, chips, cakes, pastries, and ice cream.
- Buy fruits that are less expensive such as apples.
- Drink skim milk.
- Limit the amounts of fats that you add to your diet.
- Eat no more than 6-10 ounces of meat a day.
- Eat whole grain breads.
- Avoid eating between meals and after the dinner hours.

Sleep

Your body needs sleep, and you must make sure that you get a good night's rest. Don't stay up all night because you don't have a job the next day. Make it a priority to go out every day and search for jobs throughout the day. This exercise in job hunting will help keep your mind and body healthy during this very trying period of time for you and your family.

Anxiety/Panic Attacks/Depression

Economic difficulties, loss of a job, and bankruptcy can all cause tremendous stress, which can lead to anxiety, panic attacks, depression, or worse. We are beginning to see signs of stress so great because of economic situations that people have committed suicide. These people are good people living their lives and, for whatever reasons, have found themselves in situations in which they feel they cannot cope with. When a person begins to have signs of depression, anxiety, panic attacks, or thoughts of suicide, he should seek help through a family doctor, a counselor, and/or a rabbi, priest, or minister. If the person does not have the financial means for professional treatment, he could talk to a trusted friend or employer.

No situation is so grave that the option of suicide should be considered. As an educator, I have attended many professional workshops over the years on the topic of suicide. A most important point that I once was told is "suicide is a permanent solution to a temporary problem." As we all know, a crisis does not last forever. When we are going through a traumatic event, it seems like it will never end. When people choose suicide, they do not realize the devastation that they will leave behind for their family, extended family, and friends. No one would want another human being to feel so badly that they would consider suicide as an option. The important point is to *get help*. Your problem is not insurmountable.

Web Sites

• AmericanHealthInsuranceyourbusiness.msnbc   • eHealth insurance
These two Web sites are excellent sources for information as well as to do comparison shopping with different insurance companies and with different types of plans. Shop around to get the best price. Each company offers a variety of different plans. You have the time so make sure you do your homework to get the cheapest with the most benefits.
• http://indeed.com   • http://craigslist.com
These two Web sites assist in helping you explore potential job openings.

Appendix A

Supermarket Worksheet Comparison Shopping

Item	Store 1	Store 2	Store 3	Store 4	Store 5
1					
2					
3					
4					
5					
6					
7					
8					
9					
10					
11					
12					
13					
14					
15					
16					
17					
18					
19					
20					
Total					
Ranking					
Difference From Highest					

Appendix B

Blank Supermarket Worksheet

Item	Store A	Store B	Store C
Total			
Difference			

Appendix B

Blank Supermarket Worksheet

Item	Store A	Store B	Store C
Total			
Difference			

Appendix B

Blank Supermarket Worksheet

Item	Store A	Store B	Store C
Total			
Difference			

Appendix C

Supermarket Worksheet

	Store	Store	Store
Items			
eggs (dozen, store brand)			
milk (skim, gallon)			
milk (2% of a gallon)			
Kraft (12 oz of sliced cheese)			
Gold Medal flour (5 lb)			
Kellogg cornflakes (18 oz)			
General Mills Cheerios (14 oz)			
Sunbeam bread (22 oz)			
Jell-O (gelatin)			
Jell-O (pudding)			
lunch meat Oscar Mayer (9 oz deli)			
Hellman's mayonnaise (32 oz)			
Kraft salad dressing (16 oz)			
Iceberg lettuce			
celery			
potatoes (white)			
apples (delicious)			
Breakstone sour cream (16 oz)			
whole chicken (Purdue)			
Minute Maid orange juice (½ gal)			
Philadelphia cream cheese (8 oz)			
Jif peanut butter (28 oz)			
Total			
Difference			

Appendix D

Pantry List

Dry Goods	Fruits
• Flour and Bisquick • Granulated Sugar, Brown, and Confectioners • Corn Meal • Oatmeal	• Apples • Lemons • Bananas • Seasonal Fruit • Raisins
Vegetables	**Canned Vegetables**
• Potatoes • Onions • Celery • Carrots • Green Pepper	• Diced Tomatoes (1 lb and 2 lb) • Tomato Sauce (8oz and 16 oz) • Tomato Paste • Cream of Mushroom Soup • Cream of Chicken Soup • Tomato Soup
Spices	**Dairy**
• Salt/Pepper • Baking Powder/Baking Soda • Bouillon Cubes (Beef and Chicken) • Seasoned Salt • Vinegar • Dry Onion Soup Mix	• Butter (Off Brand Acceptable) • Eggs • Sliced American Cheese • Block Sharp Cheese • Milk
Oils	**Pasta and Dried Beans**
• Olive Oil • Canola Oil • Spray Pam • Crisco/Shortening	• Vermicelli, Spaghetti, Linguine • Elbow Macaroni, Shells, Bowties, Twists • Dried Beans (Lima, Navy, Kidney, Split Pea, Northern Bean, Barley • Rice (Brown and White)

Meats	Desserts
• Hot Dogs	• Pudding/Jell-O
• Canned Tuna	• Graham Crackers/Vanilla Wafers
• Canned Chicken	• Ice Cream
• Frozen Chicken	• Cool Whip
• Frozen Hamburger	• Animal Crackers
Frozen Vegetables	**Staples**
• Peas	• Peanut Butter
• Green Beans (Cut and French Style)	• Mustard
• Corn	• Jelly
• Spinach	• Ketchup

Appendix D

Pantry List

Dry Goods	Fruits
• Flour and Bisquick • Granulated Sugar, Brown, and Confectioners • Corn Meal • Oatmeal	• Apples • Lemons • Bananas • Seasonal Fruit • Raisins
Vegetables	**Canned Vegetables**
• Potatoes • Onions • Celery • Carrots • Green Pepper	• Diced Tomatoes (1 lb and 2 lb) • Tomato Sauce (8oz and 16 oz) • Tomato Paste • Cream of Mushroom Soup • Cream of Chicken Soup • Tomato Soup
Spices	**Dairy**
• Salt/Pepper • Baking Powder/Baking Soda • Bouillon Cubes (Beef and Chicken) • Seasoned Salt • Vinegar • Dry Onion Soup Mix	• Butter (Off Brand Acceptable) • Eggs • Sliced American Cheese • Block Sharp Cheese • Milk
Oils	**Pasta and Dried Beans**
• Olive Oil • Canola Oil • Spray Pam • Crisco/Shortening	• Vermicelli, Spaghetti, Linguine • Elbow Macaroni, Shells, Bowties, Twists • Dried Beans (Lima, Navy, Kidney, Split Pea, Northern Bean, Barley • Rice (Brown and White)

Meats	Desserts
• Hot Dogs	• Pudding/Jell-O
• Canned Tuna	• Graham Crackers/Vanilla Wafers
• Canned Chicken	• Ice Cream
• Frozen Chicken	• Cool Whip
• Frozen Hamburger	• Animal Crackers
Frozen Vegetables	**Staples**
• Peas	• Peanut Butter
• Green Beans (Cut and French Style)	• Mustard
• Corn	• Jelly
• Spinach	• Ketchup

Appendix E

Coupon Organizer Labels

Beverages	Beverages
Bread and Crackers	Bread and Crackers
Cleaning Products	Cleaning Products
Dairy	Dairy
Fruits	Fruits
Meats	Meats
Miscellaneous	Miscellaneous
Paper Products	Paper Products
Snacks	Snacks
Toiletries	Toiletries
Vegetables	Vegetables

Appendix E

Coupon Organizer Labels
(copy 2)

Beverages	Beverages
Bread and Crackers	Bread and Crackers
Cleaning Products	Cleaning Products
Dairy	Dairy
Fruits	Fruits
Meats	Meats
Miscellaneous	Miscellaneous
Paper Products	Paper Products
Snacks	Snacks
Toiletries	Toiletries
Vegetables	Vegetables

Appendix F

Greeting Card Labels
(Alphabetical Organizer)

Anniversary	Anniversary
Baby	Baby
Birthday/Child	Birthday/Child
Birthday/Female	Birthday/Female
Birthday/Male	Birthday/Male
Birthday/Relative	Birthday/Relative
Congratulations	Congratulations
Encouragement	Encouragement
Engagement	Engagement
Friendship	Friendship
Get Well	Get Well
Graduation	Graduation
Holiday	Holiday
New Home	New Home

Appendix F

Greeting Card Labels
(Alphabetical Organizer continued)

Notes/Male	Notes/Male
Relative	Relative
Religious Celebrations	Religious Celebrations
Retirement	Retirement
Sympathy	Sympathy
Thank You	Thank You
Thinking of You	Thinking of You
Wedding	Wedding
Wedding Shower	Wedding Shower

Appendix G

Worksheet for
Comparison Pricing Between
Child and Adult Meals
At Fast-Food Restaurants

Fast Foods Restaurant	Adult Meal	Cost	Child's Meal	Cost	Cost Difference

Appendix H

Needs and Wants Daily Log for One Week

Use this table to make a list of all the expenditures that you make for one week. Indicate the date, the item, and how much it cost. At the end of the week, identify whether the purchase was a real need or just a want. Add the needs and the wants to determine how much they total. At this point, you will be able to determine how much money you have spent unnecessarily throughout the week.

Weekly Log of Expenditures

Date	Item	Cost	Need	Want

Date	Item	Cost	Need	Want

Appendix H

Use this table to make a list of all the expenditures that you make for one week. Indicate the date, the item, and how much it cost. At the end of the week, identify whether the purchase was a real need or just a want. Add the needs and the wants to determine how much they total. At this point, you will be able to determine how much money you have spent unnecessarily throughout the week.

Weekly Log of Expenditures

Date	Item	Cost	Need	Want

Index

A

air-conditioning, 112–13, 115
American workforce, 19
annuity, 136
anxiety, 45, 142
appetizers, 67
Asset allocation, 135–36
assets, 133, 136
auctions, 6, 97–99

B

bankruptcy, 17, 24, 44, 119, 140, 142
bargains, 40, 94–95, 97–98. *See also* yard
sales
bartering, 6, 27, 42, 107
batter, 72–73
beef
corned, 76
lean ground, 68
potpie, 61–62
See also chicken potpie
stew, 60–61, 76
See also chicken stew
biscuit, 58, 61, 69–70, 84, 103
bond, 133, 136–37
treasury, 137
bouillon cubes, 64, 75–76, 78
bread, 28–29, 31, 38, 53, 55, 69, 83–84
brown rice, 52, 63
buddy shopping, 11, 30, 33, 36–38, 40, 43,
62, 85, 91, 94–96, 101
budgets, 23, 43, 120
butter, 52, 62, 77, 83, 87
buying
car, 105, 129
house, 23, 97, 130, 135

C

cabbage, 26, 76, 82
calories, 67, 103
carpools, 7, 44, 111
cash, 130, 136
casserole, 42, 59, 64, 66, 74, 78
stuffed-ham, 66
See also soup, stuffed-ham
tuna, 78
See also tuna pâté
Cat Creek Quiche, 74
Catholic faith, 25, 32, 34–35, 137, 145
celery, 55–56, 60–62, 82
check, 40, 72, 88, 91, 97, 110, 112–13, 115,
129
chicken, 53–59, 63–64, 67
à la king, 58
back, 56, 75
baked, 53, 55–56, 59, 64, 67
breast, 55, 67, 89, 102
broth, 56–59, 66, 75, 83, 89–90
legs, 55, 90
noodles, 57, 59, 64, 75, 78
potpie, 58
See also beef potpie
stew, 57–58
See also beef stew
thighs, 89–90, 102
whole, 55, 59, 90, 102
wings, 55–56, 90, 102
chicken-salad cracker spread, 67
chili, 53, 67, 80, 90, 108
Chow Mein, 57, 78
city, 15, 23–24, 26–29, 39, 112
clothing, 15, 24, 94–95, 97, 100, 110
Cobra, 8, 139
coffee, 102, 105, 131–32